Irish Popular Superstitions

by W.R. Wilde

with an introduction by Dahlia V. Nightly

CREDITS & ACKNOWLEDGEMENTS

Wrap-Around Cover -
Beltany Ancient Standing Stone Circle – Donegal by Gareth Wray
[CC BY-SA 4.0 - https://creativecommons.org/licenses/by-sa/4.0],
via Wikimedia Commons

Black Books Logo -
Candle Collection by VectorPocket, via FreePik.com *(Cropped)*
Vanitas [Painting] by Bartholomäus Bruyn the Elder, Public Domain *(Cropped)*
Marbled Pedestal with Old Books by Kues1, via FreePik.com (Cropped)

Research / Sources -
Wikimedia Commons
www.Commons.Wikimedia.org

Many thanks to all the incredible photographers, artists,
researchers, and archivists who share their great work.

PLEASE NOTE :
As with all reprinted books of this age that are intended to perfectly reproduce the
original edition, considerable pains and effort had to be undertaken to correct fading and
sometimes outright damage to existing proofs of this title. At times, this task can be quite
monumental, requiring an almost total rebuilding of some pages from digital proofs of
multiple copies. Despite this, imperfections still sometimes exist in the final proof and
may detract slightly from the visual appearance of the text.

DISCLAIMER :
Due to the age of this book, some methods or practices may have been deemed unsafe or
unacceptable in the interim years. In utilizing the information herein, you do so at your
own risk. We republish antiquarian books without judgment or revisionism, solely for
their historical and cultural importance, and for educational purposes.

Introduction...

At *Black Books* we are so pleased to bring you another fantastic old book on myth and superstition in *Ye Olde Ireland*.

This special edition of **Irish Popular Superstitions** was written by W.R. Wilde, and first published in 1852, making it over 165 years old.

This antiquarian text explores old superstitions and folk stories of Ireland like *How to Prove a Man Mad, Effect of the Potato Failure on the Popular Mind, Superstition : The Poetry of the People, Fairies as They Were, The Poor-House, The May-Day Festival in Ireland, Secret Societies, Belteine and the Book of Rights*, and more.

The book also delves into rites and ceremonies around Holidays including Easter, *Michaelmas, Shrovetide, St. Valentine's Day, Christmas, Easter,* and *Beltane,* among others.

Irish Popular Superstitions is written with a nostalgic eye, and talks about these myths and legends being all-but forgotten, even in the time it was written. The author seems to long for a little more magic in daily life, and a sprinkle of the fantastic to temper our sophisticated cynicism.

All enthusiasts of Irish History and Superstitions in particular, and all those who are interested in old Folklore in general.

Strangely yours...

~ *Dahlia V. Nightly*

State of Jefferson, July 2018

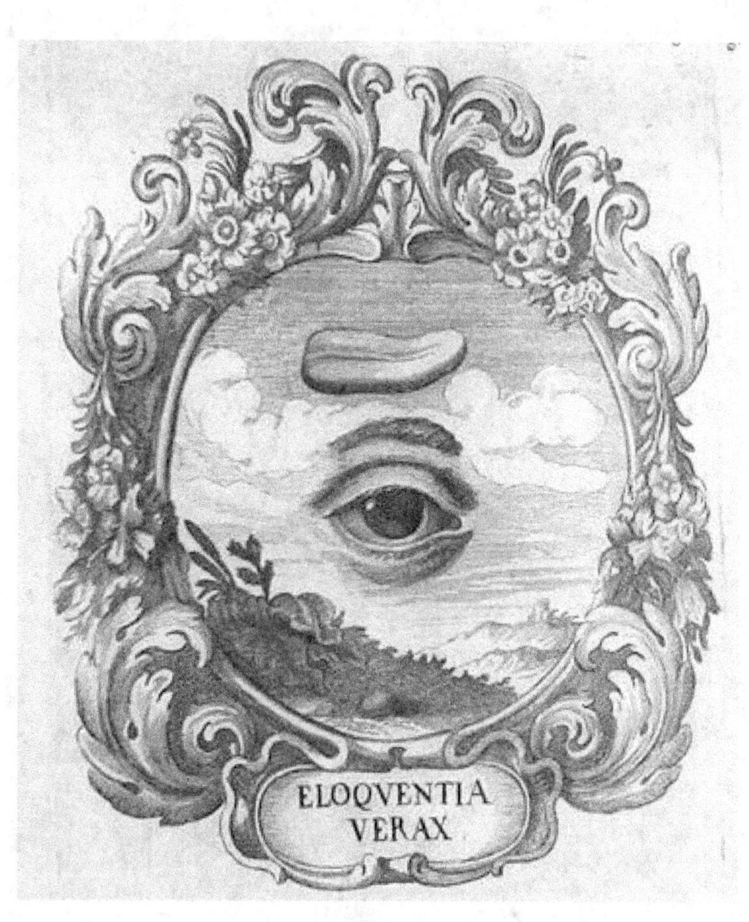
ELOQVENTIA
VERAX

La

Speranza.

PREFACE.

HAD not Shakespere embalmed in the "Midsummer Night's Dream" the Popular Superstitions and Fairy lore current in England at the time of Elizabeth, the present generation could form but a very faint idea of the ancient belief of our forefathers in the witcheries of their sylvan deities and household gods. In this utilitarian age it would be superfluous to discuss, or even to enumerate, the causes which have combined to obliterate this poetry of the people in England; suffice it to say, that it has gradually vanished before the spread of education, and the rapid growth of towns and manufactories.

A wild and daring spirit of adventure—a love of legendary romance—a deep-rooted belief in the supernatural—an unconquerable reverence for ancient customs, and an extensive superstitious creed has, from the earliest times, belonged to the Celtic race. We cannot, therefore, wonder that among the but partially civilized, because neglected and uneducated, yet withal chivalrous inhabitants of a large portion of Ireland, a belief in the marvellous should linger even to the present day. It is, however—and chiefly from the causes enumerated in the first chapter of this little work—rapidly becoming obliterated; never to return. When now I enquire after the old farmer who conducted me, in former years, to the ruined Castle or Abbey, and told me the story of its early history and inhabitants, I hear that he died during the famine. On asking for the peasant who used to sit with me in the ancient

Rath, and recite the Fairy legends of the locality, the answer is: " He is gone to America;" and the old woman who took me to the Blessed Well, and gave me an account of its wondrous cures and charms—" Where is she ? "——" Living in the Workhouse."

These legendary tales and Popular Superstitions have now become the history of the past—a portion of the traits and characteristics of other days. Will their recital revive their practice? No! Nothing contributes more to uproot superstitious rites and forms than to print them ; to make them known to the many instead of leaving them hidden among, and secretly practised by the few.

These tales form part of a large collection made for my amusement many years ago, or which were remembered since my boyhood, and they have been written as a relaxation from severer toil. Several of them have already appeared in the "Dublin University Magazine." They are now collected and presented to the public in their present form, chiefly in the hope of eliciting information from those who may be further acquainted with such matters; for which purpose I have here subjoined a list of Queries, on which I should like to have answers from my country readers. I have also added a copious index of both names and subjects, which will, I trust, likewise assist in bringing forth new matter. Should this little volume be acceptable, it will be followed by another when time permits.

QUERIES.

Popular Superstitions Generally.

Popular Belief among the Peasantry as to the Existence of Fairies, Fairy Legends, Fairy-Stricken People and Cattle; with Charms and Cures against such; Elf-darts, Crystals.

Fairy Lore, Enchantment, Witchcraft, the Evil Eye, and Fairy Abduction.

Herb Cures and Fairy Doctors, Love Charms.

Ancient Customs, Traditions, Folk's Lore, and Proverbs Relating to Superstitious Practices.

Popular Games and Pastimes, with the Rhymes and Recitations used thereat.

Legends Relating to Ancient Forts and Raths, Crosses, Bawns, Blessed Wells, and Old Burial Places.

The Non-Religious Rites and Ceremonies Relating to Births, Marriages, and Deaths.

Ceremonials Used with a Corpse, and the Forms, Plays, Rhymes, and Keens, employed at Wakes; Ceremonies used at Funerals and in Grave Yards.

Popular Cures for Diseases, particularly Madness, Bite of a Mad Dog, the King's Evil, Falling Sickness, Fever, Jaundice, Wild-fire, Warts, Childbed, Chincough, and Ague, &c.

QUERIES.

The Moon ;—Rhymes, Superstitions, and Proverbs, relating to.

Prophecies, Curses and Maledictions.

Ceremonies and Popular Usages Respecting Land, and the Preservation of Crops as well as Cattle, Milk, and Butter.

Legends and Superstitions Relating to Lakes and Rivers, with the fabulous Animals said to inhabit them.

Charms Employed against Various Disasters, Sudden Death, Drowning, &c.

Opinions with Regard to Fetches, Ghosts, and Spirits, Supernatural Appearances.

Ideas, Proverbs, and Rhymes current among the Peasantry respecting Different Animals, especially Hares, Weasels, Cats, Rooks, Wildgeese, Cocks, Wrens, Starlings, the Magpie, Raven, Waterwagtail, the Cuckoo, Robin, Dordeel, Mankeeper, Cricket, &c.

Charms appertaining to the Dead Man's Hand.

Rites and Ceremonies used at the following Festivals :—New Year's Day, Twelfth Night, Candlemas and St. Bridget's, Shrovetide, St. Valentine's Day, Easter, Whitsuntide, May Day, St. John's Eve, Garlic or Garland Sunday, Palm Sunday, Lady Day, Holy Eve, St. Martin's, Michaelmas, Christmas, St. Stephen's Day, &c., &c.

IRISH POPULAR SUPERSTITIONS.

CHAPTER I.

Revolution in Irish Peasant's Life : its Causes and Effects—Obliteration of Superstitions—Introduction of Darby Doolin—Loss of the Gentry—the Irish Pantheon—Tenant's Rights and Taxes—Demolition of the Popular and Rural Pastimes—The Ordnance Survey—Effect of the Potato Failure on the Popular Mind—Emigration and Patriotism—Who is to be the Buyer?—What we are, What we may be, and What we ought to be—The Way to Learn English—How to Prove a Man Mad—Quacks—The Last of the Superstitions.

BY the sarcasm of his Don Quixote, Cervantes, it is said, first threw ridicule upon the followers of Amadis de Gaul, checked the spirit of knight-errantry, and in fact sneered away the chivalry of Spain.   No doubt the effect produced by that work was sudden and decisive; the period, however, was propitious; light was beginning to shine out from the surrounding darkness, and the people to whom the work was addressed were learned enough to read, and had sufficient wisdom and common sense to appreciate its value, and also wit quick and ready to perceive its point.   Rapid as, it is said, was the spread of this revolution of opinion in the Peninsula, and, indeed, throughout civilized Europe generally, it was nothing, in comparison to that which has taken place, and is still going forward, in matters of belief, and popular prejudice, and national opinion, in Ireland.

The great convulsion which society of all grades here has lately experienced, the failure of the potato crop, pestilence, famine, and a most unparalleled extent of emigration, together with bankrupt landlords, pauperizing poor-laws, grinding officials, and decimating workhouses, have broken up the very foundations of social intercourse, have swept away the established theories of political economists, and uprooted many of our long-cherished opinions. In some places, all the domestic usages of life have been outraged; the tenderest bonds of kindred have been severed, some of the noblest and holiest feelings of human nature have been blotted from the heart, and many of the finest, yet firmest links which united the various classes in the community have been rudely burst asunder. Even the ceremonial of religion has been neglected, and the very rites of sepulture, the most sacred and enduring of all the tributes of affection or respect, have been neglected or forgotten; the dead body has rotted where it fell, or formed a scanty meal for the famished dogs of the vicinity, or has been thrown, without prayer or mourning, into the adjoining ditch. The hum of the spinning-wheel has long since ceased to form an accompaniment to the colleen's song; and that song itself, so sweet and fresh in cabin, field, or byre, has scarcely left an echo in our glens, or among the hamlets of our land. The Shannaghic and the Callegh in the chimney corner, tell no more the tales and legends of other days. Unwaked, *unkeened*, the dead are buried, where Christian burial has at all been observed; and the ear no longer catches the mournful cadence of the wild Irish cry, wailing on the blast, rising up to us from the valleys, or floating along the winding river, when

> "The skies, the fountains, every region near,
> Seemed all one mutual cry."

The fire on the peasant's hearth was quenched, and its comforts banished, even before his roof-tree fell, while the remnant of the hardiest and most stalwart of the people crawl about, listless spectres, unable or unwilling to rise out of their despair. In this state of things, with depopulation the most terrific which any country ever experienced, on the one hand, and the spread of education, and the introduction of railroads, colleges, industrial and other educational schools, on the other,—together with the rapid decay of the Irish vernacular, in which most of our legends, romantic tales, ballads, and bardic annals, the vestiges of Pagan rites, and the relics of fairy charms were preserved,—can superstition, or if superstitious belief, can superstitious practices continue to exist?

But these matters of popular belief and folks'-lore, these rites and legends, and superstitions, were after all, *the poetry of the people*, the bond that knit the peasant to the soil, and cheered and solaced many a cottier's fireside. Without these, on the one side, and without proper education and well-directed means of partaking of and enjoying its blessings, on the other, and without rational amusement besides, he will, and must, and has in many instances, already become a perfect brute. The rath which he revered has been, to our knowledge, ploughed up, the ancient thorn which he reverenced has been cut down, and the sacred well polluted, merely in order to uproot his prejudices, and efface his superstition. Has he been improved by such desecration of the landmarks of the past, objects which, independent of their natural beauty, are often the surest footprints of history? We fear not.

"Troth, sir," said Darby Doolin, an old Connaughtman of our acquaintance, when lately conversing upon the subject, "what betune them national boords, and godless colleges, and other sorts of larnin', and the loss of the pratey, and the sickness, and all the people that's goin' to 'Merica, and the crathurs that's forced to go into the workhouse, or is dyin' off in the ditches, and the clargy settin' their faces agin them, and tellin' the people not to give *in* to the likes, sarra wan of the *Gintry* (cross about us!) 'ill be found in the counthry, nor a word about them or their doin's in no time."

The reader must not from this suppose that our friend Darby in any way commiserated or sympathized with the bankrupt landed gentry, or felt " sore or sorry " that the landlord and the noble were, *en masse*, reduced to the same condition that the merchant, the trader, or the professional man, are, from day to day. Oh, no! These were not the people honest Darby alluded to. Small blame to him if he had but little personal acquaintance with such gentry; for " few of them ever stood in the street, or darkened the doors " of the cottages of his native village of Kilmucafaudeen.   Darby Doolin's gentry were, a short time ago at least, *resident*, and transacted their own business without either attorney, money-broker, agent, keeper, driver, or pound-keeper; they seldom visited London, and much more rarely Paris, or the Brunnens of Nassau; and though reputedly *lucky*, were scarcely ever known to frequent the gambling-table or the horse-race, but lived "in pace and quietness at home, in the ould ancient habitations of the counthry," riding by night up and down upon the moonbeams, changing their residences or localities with the whirlwind; creeping into the russet acorn shells; sleeping in summer in the purple pendent bells of the foxglove or the wild campanula; quaffing the Maydew from the gossamer threads of the early morning, and living a merry, social life, singing, dancing, and playing, with wild Eolian music, by the streamlet's bank, upon the green hill side, or round the grassy fort. And though they neither canted nor dispossessed, never took nor demanded "male or malt," head-rent, quit-rent, crown-rent, dues or duties, county-cess, parish-cess, tithes, priest's dues, poor rates, rates in aid, driverage, poundage, nor murder-money;[*] employed neither sheriffs, magistrates, barony constables, bailiffs, keepers, drivers, auctioneers, tax-collectors, process-servers, guagers, spies, potteen-hussars, police, nor standing army; passed no promissory notes, and served neither notices to quit, ejectments, nor civil bills, they exacted from the people a reverence and a respect such as few potentates, civil, military, or ecclesiastical, could ever boast of.

In most of the leases made in the county of Galway, even twenty years ago,—and we believe the practice was common in other parts of Ireland also,—there was, besides the ordinary rent, a covenant for so many pullets, geese and turkeys, so many days' work in spring and harvest, and so many pounds of grey yarn thread.   These remnants of the feudal system were termed "duties."   The agent, the tithe-proctor, the driver also, and the pound-keeper, had each his dues.   Independent of the ordinary

---

[*] It is but too fully established that in most instances of agrarian murder, the whole townland was compelled to contribute to the price paid for the bloody deed, or heavily taxed to support the murderer, or pay his passage to America.

legal fees of the latter functionary, there were others which he obtained in this wise. If a man's cow was in pound, and his family in want of its support, he went to the pound-keeper to get it back, until the day of the *cant;* instead of leaving it starving, and up to its middle in mud in the pound for a fortnight, he paid the fee. The cattle-jailer took out a piece of paper, the leaf of a book, or the back of a letter—anything, in fact, having printed or written characters upon it—laid it down on the road, and the owner of the beast taking it up, pledged himself upon it to deliver up the animal within the appointed time. Rarely, indeed, was the pledge ever known to be broken, although many a serious riot and attempt at rescue had been made on the first capture of the beast.

"True for you," says Darby, "they are going fast, that *gentle* race (the Lord be with them!) but sure you wouldn't have them wait, them that were always an *out-door* population, to be taken by the scruff of the neck and sent by the guardians and commissioners just to try their feet on the flure of the poorhouse,* or be shot down like thrushes, as the boys at Ballingarry were. The *good people* are leaving us fast : nobody ever hears now the tic-tac of the *leprechaun,* or finds the cute little chap with his Frenchman's hat and yellow breeches, sated on a boochalaun bwee of a summer's morning, with lab-stone on knee, and hammer in hand, tick-tack, tick-tack, welting soles and lasting brogues for his elfin brethren. God be with the time when Donall-na-Trusslog (Daniel of the leaps), met the leprechaun one morning on Rahona bog, with the *adhaster buidhe* (golden bridle, which, whenever shaken, was found with the yellow steed attached to it) in the one hand, and the *sporran-na-skillinge* (the purse that was never without a shilling) in the other. He laid hold of him, and swore that he should never part him till he had given up these treasures. ' Yarrah,' said the little fellow, ' what good is it for you to get them, when that fellow behind you will immediately take them from you ?'

---

* We lately expostulated with one of our old beggars as to why she did not go into the poor-house—" Arrah, sure agra, I wouldn't be alive a week in it; I that's ate up with the rheumatics; troth, I went there the other day, jist to try my feet on the flure, and I wouldn't be alive in it a week," was the graphic reply.

Daniel gave one of his sudden circuitous leaps, but on his turning again to the little fellow, he found, to his eternal grief, that he had scampered off, and was grinning at him from the spray of a bucky briar in the neighbouring hedgerow.

"Sure the children wouldn't know anything about the *pooca* but for the story of the blackberries after Michaelmas.* The warning voice of the *banshee* is mute; for there are but few of the 'rale ould stock' to mourn for now; the *sheogue* and the *thirish* are every year becoming scarcer; and even the harmless *linane shie* † is not talked about now-a-days, and does not hold discourse with e'er a fairy woman in the whole barony,—them that were as plenty as lumpers afore the yellow male came amongst us, and made us as wake and as small as a north country rushlight, or a ha'penny herring.‡ No lie to say the times are altered; sure the snow and the frost itself is lavin' us." Darby Doolin writes us word (for he is a mighty knowledgeable man, and fit to plade with a barrister`,§ that all the stories about the fairies and the pishogues are going fast, and will soon be lost to us and our heirs for ever.

The old forms and customs, too, are becoming obliterated; the festivals are unobserved, and the rustic festivities neglected or forgotten; the bowlings, the cakes and the prinkums‖ (the

---

* It is a popular belief—kept up probably to prevent children eating them when over ripe—that the *pooca*, as he rides over the country, defiles the blackberries at Michaelmas and Holly-eve.

† These various personages, and the ideas attached to them, will be explained during the course of these papers. The representation of the "The Lianhan Shee," as given by Carleton, in his "Traits and Stories," does not hold good in the west, where that familiar spirit is looked upon as a much more innoxious attendant of the fairy woman. The leprechaun, or clurichaun, as he is termed in Munster, and the banshee and phooka, or pooca, the Puck of Shakspeare, are already known, even to English readers. The sheeogue is the true fairy; thivishes or thoushas (shadowy apparitions) are literally ghosts; and pisherogues, or pishogues, a term used both in the Irish manuscripts and in the vernacular, means properly witchcraft or enchantment.

‡ The *laffeen scuddaun*, or halfpenny herring, is often used as a term of insignificance.

§ By the term "barrister," the Irishman does not mean a lawyer generally, but the county assistant barrister, who is held in great veneration. In Ireland we have the lawyer, the councillor, and the barrister.

‖ In Connaught, in former times, when a dance was held on a Sunday evening at a cross-roads, or any public place of resort, a large cake, like what is called a peasants' balls and routs), do not often take place when starvation and pestilence stalk over a country, many parts of which appear as if a destroying army had but recently passed through it. Such is the desolation which whole districts, of Connaught at least, at this moment present; entire villages being levelled to the ground, the fences broken, the land untilled and often unstocked, and miles of country lying idle and unproductive, without the face of a human being to be seen upon it. The hare has made its form on the hearth, and the lapwing wheels over the ruined cabin. The faction-fights, the hurlings, and the mains of cocks that used to be fought at Shrovetide and Easter, with such other innocent amusements, are past and gone these twenty years, and the mummers and May-boys left off when we were a gossoon no bigger than a pitcher. It was only, however, within those three years that the *waits* ceased to go their rounds upon the cold frosty mornings in our native village at Christmas; and although the "wran boys" still gather a few halfpence on St. Stephen's Day, we understand there wasn't a candle blessed in the chapel, nor a *breedogue* * seen in the barony where Kilmucafauden stands, last Candlemas Day; no, nor even a cock killed in every fifth house, in honour of St. Martin; and you'd step over the *brosnach*† of a bonfire that the childer lighted last St. John's Eve.

barnbrack, with a variety of apocryphal birds, fabulous fishes, and outlandish quadrupeds, such as are only known in heraldic zoology, raised in bold relief on its upper crust, was placed on the top of a churn-dash, and tied over with a clean white cloth; the staff of the churn-dash was then planted outside the door as a sign of the fun and amusement going on within. When they had danced and drank their fill, the *likeliest* boy took the prettiest colleen, and led her out to the cake, and placed it in her hands as Queen of the Feast; it was then divided among the guests, and the festivities continued. The word *prinkum* is sometimes used in the county Galway, to express a great rout or merry-making, in which dancing, courting, coshering, whisky-drinking, card-playing, fighting, and sometimes a little ribbonism, form the chief diversions.

* The *breedogue* was an image of St. Bridget, generally styled by the country girls "Miss Biddy" It was carried about on the 1st of February. As one of the objects of this little work is to record the "humours" and ceremonials of this and other like festivals, formerly observed in Ireland, it is unnecessary to enter further into their description in the notes to the present chapter.

† The term *brosnach* is generally applied to an armful or an apronful of sticks used for firing; it literally means a bundle of rotten sticks for firing. A brusna of furze is carried on the back.

The native humour of the people is not so rich and racy as in days of yore; the full round laugh does not now bubble up from the heart of the Irish girl when making her toilet at the wayside pool, nor the joke pass from the pedlar or bagman to the pig-driver as they trudge alongside of one another to fair or market. Well, honoured be the name of Theobald Mathew —but, after all, a power of fun went away with the whiskey. The spirits of the people is n't what they were when a man could get drunk for three halfpence, and find a sod on a kippeen * over the door of every second cabin in the parish, from Balloughoiage bridge to the town of Glan. The pilgrimages formerly undertaken to holy wells and sacred shrines for cures and penances have been strenuously interdicted; the wells themselves neglected, the festival days of their saints passed by, and their virtues forgotten; their legends, too, often of great interest to the topographer and historian, and many of which were recounted by the bards and annalists of earlier times, are untold; and the very sites of many of these localities are at present unknown. The fairies, the whole pantheon of Irish demigods are retiring, one by one, from the habitations of man to the distant islands where the wild waves of the Atlantic raise their foaming crests, to render their fastnesses inaccessible to the schoolmaster and the railroad engineer; or they have fled to the mountain passes, and have taken up their abodes in those wild romantic glens—lurking in the gorgeous yellow furze and purple heath, amidst the savage disruptured rocks, or creeping beneath the warrior's grave, learnedly, but erroneously, called the Druid Crumlegh—where the legend preserved by the antiquary, or the name transmitted by the topographer, alone marks their present habitation. When the peasant passes through these situations now he forgets to murmur the prayer which was known to preserve from harm those who trod the paths of the " good people," and, by thrusting his thumb between his fore and middle finger, to make the sign of the cross—indeed, he scarcely remembers to cross himself at all; and in a few years to come the localities of the fairies will be

* A sod of turf stuck on a sally switch or kippeen, and placed in the thatch of an Irish cabin, is the sign of " good liquor within."

altogether forgotten. The wild strains of aërial music which floated round the ancient rath, and sung the matin and the vesper of the shepherd boy, who kept his flocks hard by, are heard no more, and the romance of elfin life is no longer recited to amuse or warn the rising peasant generation. To the log-house by the broad waters of the Ohio or the Missisippi, to the wild monotonous Australian prairie, or even to the golden soil of California, the emigrant has carried the fairy lore of the mother country; so that, to the charming descriptions of our countrywoman, Mrs. Hall—to the traits and stories of William Carleton—the happy illustration of Irish manners by Banim and Gerald Griffin—the pencillings of Lady Chatterton, or the graphic sketches of Cæsar Otway and Samuel Lover—but, above all, to the Munster legends, embalmed by Crofton Croker, must the enquirer after fairy lore refer, who would seek for information on such matters in Ireland twenty years to come.*

Would that the Irish emigrant carried with him his super-stitions only. But no. In the rankling hatred towards the English rule in Ireland—increased by the very circum-stances under which so many of our countrymen now quit our shores, fostered and transmitted unalloyed for generations to a foreign soil—has future England more to fear from future America in case of national war, than all the rebellions and agitations which puny Ireland could possibly excite, now or hereafter.

The ordnance survey, of which we feel so justly proud, is a

---

* The best of all our fairy tales are, perhaps, the " Superstitions of the Irish Peasantry," in the volumes of the " London and Dublin Magazine," published from 1825 to 1828. "The Newry Magazine," and " Bolster's Cork Magazine," also contain much interesting information on this subject.

One of our most learned and observant Roman Catholic friends has just writ-ten to us, in answer to some queries relative to superstitions—"The tone of society in Ireland is becoming more and more *Protestant* every year; the literature is a Protestant one, and even the priests are becoming more Protestant in their conversation and manners. They have condemned all the holy wells and resorts of pilgrims, with the single exception of Lough Derg, and of this they are ashamed: for, whenever a Protestant goes upon the Island, the ceremonies are stopped! Among all the affectionate mentions of his dearly-beloved father made by John O'Connell, he had not the courage to say '*the Lord rest his sowle.*' I have watched these changes with great interest."

case in point. It was commenced in 1825, and finished a few years ago. Eminent scholars, well acquainted with the language and habits of the people, and educated up to the point required, traversed the country in all directions, talked with, and lived among the people, for the purpose of fixing ancient boundaries, testing the accuracy and value of ancient documents, and collecting that great amount of traditional, antiquarian, and topographical information which our ordnance records at present embody; while another class of men were occupied at home in arranging, collating, testing with ancient Gaelic manuscripts, and finally preserving the information transmitted to them by the former. Could the materials then obtained be collected now? No. We may confidently appeal to Larcom, Petrie, O'Donovan, Curry, and other eminent men employed upon that great national work, for the truth of this assertion.

The dynasties of Europe have been shaken; many of the most ancient governments overthrown; and the whole of the continent convulsed with internal strife, or shaken by sudden change as the late tempest of revolution swept along its plains and leaped over its mountain tops. The very Pope himself, the head of the most widely-spread and numerous sect of Christians in the world, has been rudely driven from the seat of St. Peter, a wanderer and an exile, though assisted by the contributions of the "*starving Irish!*" and in all probability his temporal power has been much abridged or even annihilated: but what are these revolutions to that which has been and is now effecting in Ireland by the failure of a single article of diet? All these countries will settle down, more or less, into the condition in which they were before 1848. Some change emperors —young ones for old—though, as in the case of Aladdin's lamp, the change may not be for the better; others discard kings, and, under the name of republicanism, enjoy presidents or dictators; parliaments appear to be the panacea with one set of people, and a scoffing disregard of excommunication the chief delight and boast of another; but in the end it will be found that they will nearly all shake down with a very little more or very little less of liberty than they had in the beginning of the year 1848.* The German will twist his moustache, smoke, and live on his beer and sour krout; and the Frenchman drink his wine at three sous a bottle, shrug his shoulders, and enjoy his *fête* as before. Not so the Irishman; all his habits and modes of life, his very nature, position, and standing in the social scale of creation, will and must be altered by the loss of his potato. Ay, even more than if he was suddenly compelled to turn Mahommedan,—changing all his chapels, churches, and meeting-houses into mosques,—or had a parliament going round with the judge of assize, and sitting in every county town in Ireland twice a-year.

"I was n't asey in myself," says our old friend Darby, "till I wrote to tell you all the doins that 's gettin' on with in the counthry, and how, if times does n't mind, I 'll sell the two little slips †—them that was bonoveens on last Lady-day—and gather in the trifle of money that 's due me out of the *gombeen*‡ these two years; and when I 've made *baton* § of the meddin, and dishposed of the cabin and the little garden to Phauric Brannach, I 'll be after takin' myself and the ould woman to the place they 're diggin' up the goold as thick as poorens ‖ used to be in harvest. Besides, I 'm noways continted at stayin' here at this present writin', and I 'm tould Colonel Browne is watching me like a tarrier after a weasel. Whisht! sure avourneen, I was out in the 'ruction in '98; and I walked all the ways to see Dan (the heavens be his bed this night!) at Tara, and bring home a sod from off the grave of the boys we planted there the night afore I ran back into Connaught—just to the ould spud,

* This assertion was printed in the " Dublin University Magazine" for May, 1849. Subsequent events have proved its truth.

† *Slip* is the term applied to a young pig, of from six months to one year old; while bonov, or bonoveen, means a piggin-riggin, or sucking-pig, or one much younger than a slip.

‡ *Gombeen* means lending out money or provisions upon an exorbitant and most usurious rate of interest; by it, however, has commenced the foundation of many a considerable fortune. A gombeen man is among the country people what the bill-broker and money-lender is among the higher classes.

§ *Baton*—skinning the land and burning it, in order to extract its utmost value as manure. Various acts of parliament are in force against this most injurious practice; but it is still had recourse to, particularly in Monaghan, to the detriment of both land and landlord.

‖ *Poreens*—small potatoes.

where your own four bones were bred and born, a one side of
Rawcroghan."

If ever there was a nation that clung to the soil, and earned
patriotism by the love of the very ground they walk on, it is
(or we may now write was) the Irish peasantry. The Jew
carries about with him from land to land a portion of the soil
of Palestine, that it may mingle with his grave.   Lately, when
the author of the " Pleasures of Hope " was interred, a deputa-
tion of the Poles of London cast into his tomb—an offering to
his genius—some earth from the grave of Kosciusko.   Not
many years ago, we stood upon the custom-house quays of
Dublin, watching a large emigrant ship, bound for St. John's,
getting under weigh.   The wind and tide were favourable ; the
captain was impatient, and the names of the passengers having
been called over, it was found that one was missing, a stout
labourer from Kilkenny, a great favourite with his neigh-
bours and fellow-passengers.   The captain swore, as captains
will on such occasions, that he would not wait a moment
for the rascal, who, he supposed, was " getting drunk " in some
of the neighbouring public-houses.* The prayers and entreaties
of his fellow-passengers were in vain ; the last plank was about
to be hauled on board, when the missing passenger rushed
breathless through the crowd towards the ship, carrying in his
hands a green sod, about as large as that used to " estate " a
lark, which he had just cut from one of the neighbouring fields.
" Well," said he, as he gained the deck, amidst the shouts of his
friends, " with the blessing of God, I 'll have this over me in the
new country."   Was not this patriotism?

There is at present a spring tide of emigration from Ireland,
and great is the rejoicing of those who imagine we are to be
benefited by it ;—the Malthusian who feared for the conse-
quences of over-population (although we are inclined to be-
lieve the country was not much over-populated as a whole,
although it certainly was most unequally populated) ; the rate-
payer, who is now paying twenty-five shillings and sixpence in

* The facetious, witty, and sarcastic Brennan was once asked at dinner,
whether he did not like to be drunk ?—" No, ma'am," was his reply, " but I like
to be *getting* drunk."

the pound! and the landlord who is buying up the small holdings for three or five pounds each, from those who "cumber the ground." Every one who can muster three pounds ten by the pledge of his crop, or for the good-will of his holding, or by "making-off" with the rent, or by any means within his power; all the able-bodied among the people, from the snug yeoman and frieze-coated cottier to the top-booted buckeen, are on the move for America, leaving us the idle and ill-conditioned, the weakly, the decrepid, the aged and the orphan, to be supported in our workhouses, or to drag out a miserable existence begging from door to door,—so that it may well be said, the heart of Ireland now beats in America. The sums of money that are returned to this country from the western continent daily, for the purpose of taking out emigrants, are quite astonishing. Not only that, but the feelings with which they leave are becoming altered. There is scarcely an observer of Irish manners, or who has mixed much among the people, that has not witnessed many heart-rending scenes at the parting of emigrants for some years past. It was not amidst the noise and bustle of the crowded quay that these outpourings of the heart could always be seen; but by the canal's banks, when the "whole country side" came to bless and bid adieu to the travellers, and crowded round at every lock and station for miles along the road, raising at times the wild Irish cry, and often forcing their way upon deck to have another last embrace. We remember many such scenes ten or twelve years ago. There was one instance, in particular, which struck us not only as characteristic of a mother's love, but of the ideas which the Irish peasantry possessed on the subject of the new continent, and of the complete earthly severing which took place when friends and relations parted on the Bog of Allen. The Royal Canal packet-boat, dragged by a pair of lazy garrauns at the rate of three miles an hour, had taken in a cargo of emigrants, principally labourers from the county of Longford. Their friends followed for a considerable distance, many, brimful of whisky as well as grief, crowding upon the bridges, and sometimes pulling the boat to the brink by the tow-rope, for the purpose of sending a message to one of their transatlantic friends,—to the great terror and no small danger of the non-emigrating passengers. All gradually fell back, except one very old woman, who, with her grey elf-locks streaming in the wind, her petticoat tucked above the knees, and her old red cloak floating free from her shoulders, still, with unabated energy, ran after the vessel which contained her only son. He was a red-headed freckled-faced *codger* of about twenty years of age, rather diminutive in size, but what is called *set* in his build, clad in a huge whitish frieze *coatha more*, corduroy smalls open at the knees, a Killamanka waist-coat, and a grinder round his neck, and with sullen looks, trembling lips, and swollen eyes, sat upon his *chist*, with his legs hanging over the side of the vessel. Whenever our speed slackened, or we came to a lock, or any impediment stopped our way, the poor woman knelt down and offered up a fervent prayer for the child she was parting with for ever, and occasionally gave him some advice as to his future conduct. At last, having invoked, with all the eloquence of frantic grief, a blessing upon his head, she cried out, " Orah, Thomasseen, don't forget to say your prayers, and never change your voice nor your colour when you go among the blacks." *

What a difference has ten years made in the feelings of the Irish peasant! He now no longer looks forward to better or happier times in his father-land; seed-time and harvest, the price of pigs or the rise of grain, enter not into his calculations; but he turns with a longing eye to his far-distant destination in the west, and he starves, and grinds, and toils, not for the good of the land which gave him birth, but to amass and husband the means which are to transport him for ever from his once-loved Erin. The friends who now accompany the band

---

* Even in the northern, and more independent and comfortable, because more educated and industrious counties, a certain season, usually in spring, was set apart for emigrating, and it was always one of mourning and lamentation. In the west, during the emigrating season, of late years, the canal company were obliged to employ police to travel with the packet-boat, in order to keep back and preserve order among the crowds which rushed on board whenever the vessel approached a landing-place. About five years ago, a frightful accident occurred upon the Royal Canal, near Dublin; the boat was overpowered by numbers both of emigrants and their friends, and sinking with great rapidity, upwards of fourteen persons were drowned.

of emigrants to the railway terminus part as if they were but
going into the next county—" Well, Jim, God be with you,
and a safe journey to you; take care of the woman that
owns you, and remember me to Biddy Sullivan. Tell her
I'll be after you agin Aesther." The bell rings, the shrill
whistle of the engine gives the warning note, and the parting
is over.*

Take care, landlords, gentlemen, and governors of Ireland.
The clearing system, if not carried too far, has been, at least,
carried on too rapidly. Had you improved the condition of the
peasantry, or even attempted to do so, some twenty years ago,
you might not have to support them in the poor-house now, nor
receive their dying malediction. You may want the labourer
yet; the English farmer also may require the aid of the *spal-
peen* before harvest is over. We will not press this subject
further, at a time when almost every hand and every pen is
raised against the landed proprietors indiscriminately, and
when, perhaps, one of our next essays may be upon the *paleon-
tology* of the Connaught estated gentry, as well as those who
reside in the butter-cups and among the raths and mounds
erected by our ancestors. [This, it must be recollected, was
written in the Spring of 1849. How truly it has turned out,
the past year proves.]

At our request, however, Darby has remained to see what
the end of all agitation,—if such a thing is possible in Ireland,
—and the next harvest may do for the country. Perhaps we
have been somewhat selfish in this respect, for, as he has long
been considered the knowingest man in the whole country, and
could tell more stories about the ould times and the " good
people," and knew more about cures and charms than " all the

---

* Considerable surprise has been excited, not only at the quantity of money
transmitted to their friends in this country by emigrants, but at the very short
time which elapsed between the period of their landing in America and the
arrival of the money-order in Ireland. It must not, however, be supposed that
the money has been all earned by the emigrant within that short space. To raise
the sum required for bringing out one or more of his family, the peasant or the
artizan—but principally the former—mortgages his labour for a certain time to
a farmer, or other employer, who, glad to procure a good workman for a certain
stipulated rate of wages, advances the necessary supply.

books that were ever shut and opened," and was up to the genealogy of all the ancient families, and had been at every bawne and coort* in Connaught as often as he had fingers and toes, we desired to preserve some of his curious lore before he crossed the Atlantic in his old age.

If, however, we cannot hope much for the future, let us for the present, at least, live in the memory of the past.

We are now in the transition state, passing through the fiery ordeal from which it is hoped we are to arise purified from laziness and inactivity, an honest, truth-telling, hard-working, industrious, murder-hating, business-minding, rent-paying, self-relying, well-clad, sober, cooking, healthy, thriving, peaceable, loyal, independent, Saxon-loving people ; engaged all day long, and every day except Sundays (though Archbishop Whately, more power to him ! would back us at a hurling on that same), in sowing and mowing, tilling and reaping, raising flax, fattening bullocks, and salting pork, or fishing and mending our nets and lobster-pots; instead of being a poor, dependent, untruthful, idle, ignorant, dirty, slinging, *sleeven*, cringing, begging set; governed by the bayonet or the bribe; generally misunderstood; always *sould* by the agitator at home, and the mimber abroad; ground down by the pauper absentee or his tyrannical agent; bullied by the petty sessions magistrates; alternately insulted and cajoled by the minister of the day, misrepresented and scandalized as Whig and Tory prevailed; bullied by the Browns and Beresfords to-day, worshiping O'Connell to-morrow ; vilified by the London press, and demoralized by charity jobbing. In fact, the most ill-used, and, to adopt the phraseology of Mr. Doolin, "the most jury-packing, road-jobbing, paper-reading, buckeen-breeding, sea-bathing, car-driving, cockle-eating, cup-tossing, tea-and-whisky-drinking, ribbon-lodging, orange-lodging, fighting, shouting, landlord-shooting, pig-jobbingest, potato-lovingest, good-for-nothingest nation on the face of the universal globe." All this is to be set aside, and all the good we have described, and more to boot is, it is said, to be brought about, and we hope to

---

* *Bawne:* an inclosed keep—an ancient castle. A modern noble residence is frequently called a coort, or court.

live to see the day it may come to pass, though we don't know exactly how it is to be effected.

Repeal is dead; its ghost was last seen at Ballingarry, but vanished in smoke and a flash of fire; some say it is hid in a cave in Slievenamon; but I don't give in to that. O'Connellism was kilt by the young Irelanders, who blew themselves up with the infernal machine with which they had arranged to shoot Dan and the sodjers. Education, emigration, Queen's colleges, Cashel synods, stopping the Maynooth grant, discriminating rates, rates in aid, and other variations in the poor-laws; soil analysis, green crops, agricultural missionaries, model-farms, manufactories, rotatory parliaments, quakers, fisheries, suspension of the habeas corpus, ecclesiastical titles bills, waste land improvements, paying the priests and putting down the establishment, arming the Orangemen, and "Peel" plantations, with a thousand other speculations, schemes, and propositions, have each their advocates. One thing, however, is certain, the great bulk of the land in the west and south must change owners; sooner or later it must come into the market either in wholesale or retail, and now the sooner the better. But who will be the buyers? Oh! Englishmen— English capital, that is what we want. "Just wait a bit;" we have been planted, replanted, and transplanted by the English and Scotch on several occasions, and in various ways; we are, it may now be said, undergoing the process of subsoil plough-ing; the great bulk of the old population in the south and west is being put *under the sod*, and we sincerely trust the noxious weeds may be got rid of in the process. Let it, however, be remembered what the country gained by these various planta-tions: the " mere Irish " were driven like wolves into the wilds and fastnesses of Donegal and Connaught, without their condi-tion being one iota improved in two centuries. The Cromwel-lian soldier has, in some instances, become the Tipperary murderer. At the Boyne this country changed masters, and the land its owners—the native Irish gentleman, the adherent of the Stuarts, was replaced by the victorious English captain or lieutenant, whose descendants are now some of the first to " go to the wall," although these persons obtained the fee of their estates merely on condition of their driving out the Celts; and as to the hired Scotch agriculturists, they never effected a single improvement outside their employer's demesne, or bettered the condition of the Irish farmer in any respect.

Well, no matter what comes, we'll lose the *gintry*, so we have made arrangement with Darby and some of our old Connaught acquaintances, aided by friends in the other provinces, to furnish us, from time to time, with a few particulars about the old customs and social antiquities of Ireland, especially such as have not already appeared, at any length, in print. It is possible, however, that we may frequently be found quoting inadvertently without acknowledgment, as the old newspapers and magazines constantly recorded instances of superstition ; and the local histories also mention many such. It would be impossible, indeed, to say how often we are making use of, without acknowledgment, the numerous contributions afforded us by our country friends.

This is, as our readers, who have been able to follow us thus far, have already perceived, rather a discursive chapter, but so is our subject, which has been taken up like the sybil's leaves, disarranged, in rags and patches, as time, opportunity, or the immediate matter in hand invited. We have already alluded to the decay of the Irish language as one of the means by which our legends and superstitions are becoming obliterated. It is scarcely possible to conceive the rapidity with which this is being effected, or the means taken to bring it about. We may relate the following incident as characteristic of the love of learning, and the spread of education among the peasantry in the west of Ireland, as well as the means forcibly employed to expunge the Gaelic as a spoken language. Some years ago we were benighted on a summer evening by the shores of Loch Ina, near the foot of those picturesque mountains, called the twelve pins of Benna-Beola, in Connemara. Our guide conducted us to a neighbouring village, where we were received for the night with that hospitality which has for ever been the characteristic of those wild mountaineers. While supper was preparing, and the potatoes laughing and steaming in the *skieh,*[*] the children gathered round to have a look at the stranger, and one of them, a little boy about eight years of age, addressed a short sentence in Irish to his sister, but meeting the father's eye, he immediately cowered back, having, to all appearance, committed some heinous fault. The man called the child to him, said nothing, but drawing forth from its dress a little stick, commonly called a scoreen or tally, which was suspended by a string round the neck, put an additional notch in it with his penknife. Upon our inquiring into the cause of this proceeding, we were told that it was done to prevent the child speaking Irish; for every time he attempted to do so a new nick was put in his tally, and when these amounted to a certain number, summary punishment was inflicted upon him by the schoolmaster. Every child in the village was similarly circumstanced, and whoever heard one of them speak a word of Irish was authorized to insert the fatal nick. We asked the father if he did not love the Irish language—indeed the man scarcely spoke any other; " I do," said he, his eye kindling with enthusiasm ; " sure it is the talk of the ould country, and the ould times, the language of my father and all that's gone before me—the speech of these mountains, and lakes, and these glens, where I was bred and born ; but you know," he continued, " the children must have larnin', and, as they tache no Irish in the National School, we must have recourse to this to instigate them to talk English." Upon further inquiry we found that the school alluded to was upwards of three miles distant, and that one of the able-bodied villagers escorted the children there each day, summer and winter, occasionally carrying the weak, and conducting the party with safety across the fords, and through some difficult passes which intervened. We have known a young man, who had assumed a very *fine* English accent, twitted with the circumstance of his having once carried the " *score*," by being told, " Arrah, leave off your English, 'tisn't so long since the beam was round your neck."

The fairy legends and traditions of the south of Ireland—the Cluricaune, the Merrow, the Duhallane, and the O'Donohues, &c., have been already faithfully described by Crofton

[*] *Skiehogue, skib, skieh,* the oval basket in which potatoes are strained.

Croker; but the subject is by no means exhausted, even in Munster; while a new set of elves, spirits, and goblin influences, with somewhat different ideas attached to each, pervade the west, particularly the counties of Mayo and Galway, and the isles which speckle the wild Atlantic along their shores—the group of Arran, Turk, Boffin, Innis Shark, Clare Island, Achill, and from Innis-Beagle to the far-famed Innis-Murray, opposite to the Sligo coast. Even when the legend common to the south or north is retained in these localities, it is in a new dress, with new dramatis personæ, and entirely new scenery, machinery, decorations, and processions ; thus, the story of Daniel O'Rourke is told upon a winter's night, by the laussogue's blaze,* in the Islands of Shark and Boffin, under the name of Terence O'Flaherty, as a warning to the stayers out late, by people who never heard of the "Munster Legends," to which we have alluded.† The phraseology of our Connaught story-teller is also different in many respects from that of the northern or Munsterman, as may be gleaned from this chapter.

But it is not in the west, or among what is termed the true Celtic population alone, that superstitions and mystic rites are still practised. We have fortune-tellers within the Circular-road of Dublin ! and fairy doctors, of repute, living but a few miles from the metropolis. Not six months ago a man was transported for ten years for so far practising upon the credulity of a comfortable family in the county of Longford, as to obtain sums of money, by making them believe he was their deceased father, who was not dead, but only among the *good people*, and permitted to return occasionally to visit his friends. While we write, a country newspaper informs us of the body of a child having been disinterred at Oran, in the County Roscommon, and its arms cut off, to be employed in the performance of certain mystic rites. About a year ago a man in the county of Kerry roasted his child to death, under the impression that it was a fairy. He was not brought to trial, as the crown prosecutor mercifully looked upon him as insane.

* *Fassogue, Lassogue,* or *sup*—a piece of dry bog-deal used as a torch.

† The story of Daniel O'Rourke appeared many years before the publication of the Munster Legends, in a periodical called the " Dundee Repository."

Madness has either been assumed, or sworn to, as a means of getting off prisoners, on more than one occasion, to our own knowledge. We remember sitting, some years ago, beside a celebrated veteran prisoner's counsel, in a county town in Connaught, who was defending a man on his trial for murder, committed apparently without provocation, in the open day, and before a number of witnesses; the prisoner having, with a heavy spade, clove through the skull of his unresisting victim. The defence intended to be set up was, as usual, an alibi. Numbers of people were ready to come forward and swear he was not, and could not be, at the place specified in the indictment at all. As the trial proceeded, however, the sagacious lawyer, entrusted with the defence, at once saw that he had not a leg to stand on, and, turning abruptly to the prisoner's attorney, swore with an oath bigger than that taken by any of the witnesses, "He'll be hanged. Could you not prove him mad?"

"Oh! yes; 'mad as a March hare.' I'll get plenty of people to prove that," was the solicitor's ready reply.

"But did you ever know of his doing anything out of the way? Now, did you ever hear of his eating his shoes, or the likes of that?"

"Shoes? I'll get 'you a man that will swear he eat a new pair of brogues, nails and all."

"Well, then," said the barrister, "put him up; and let us get our dinner."

The attorney retired to look after his witnesses, while a prolonged cross-examination of one of the prosecutors then upon the table, enabled the "sharp practitioner" to alter his tactics and prepare for the defence. Accordingly, the very first witness produced for the defence swore to the insanity of the prisoner; and the intelligent jury believing in the truth of the brogue-eating, including the digestion of tips, heel-taps, sole-nails, squares, tacks, sprigs, hangups, pavours and sparables, acquitted the prisoner! He was about to be discharged from the dock, when the judge committed him to a lunatic asylum.

During a recent assizes, in one of the southern counties, a witness, who prevaricated not a little, was rather roughly interrogated in her cross-examination, as to the nature of an oath, and the awful consequences of breaking it. "Do you know, my *good* girl," thundered the crown lawyer, " what would happen to you if you perjured yourself?"

" Troth, I do well, sir," said she ; " I wouldn't get my expinses."

There are certain types of superstition common to almost all countries in similar states of progress or civilization, and others which abound in nearly every condition of society ; and strange to say, what was science—written, ackowledged, and accepted science—not more than two centuries ago, is now pronounced vulgar error and popular superstition. It would, no doubt, form a subject of great interest to trace back our traditional antiquities, and to compare them one with another—the German and Scandinavian with the Irish, Scotch, or English—those of the western and eastern continents generally, with the rites and ceremonies, or opinions, of which vestiges still exist among ourselves ; when, indeed, strange affinities and similarities would be found to obtain among the North American Indians, and the Burmese and other Orientals, with those even yet practised in the Irish highlands and islands; but this would be a laborious task, and unsuited to the pages of our work, or to the popular elucidation of our fairy lore.

Of all superstitions, the medical lingers longest, perhaps, because the incentive to its existence must remain, while disease, real or imaginary—either that capable of relief, or totally incurable—continues to afflict mankind, and, therefore, in every country, no matter how civilized, the quack, the mountebank, the charm-worker, and the medico-religious impostor and nostrum-vendor, will find a gullable, *payable* public to prey upon. The only difference between the water-doctor living in his schloss, the mesmeriser practising in the lordly hall, or the cancer and the consumption curer of the count or duchess, spending five thousand a-year in advertisements, paid into the queen's exchequer, who drives his carriage and lives in Soho-square, and the " medicine man " of the Indian, or the " knowledgeable woman " of the half-savage islander, residing in a hut cut out of the side of a bog-hole, or formed in the cleft of a granite rock, is, that the former are almost invariably wilful impostors, and the latter frequently believe firmly in the efficacy of their art, and often refuse payment for its exercise.

CHAPTER II.

THE MAY-DAY FESTIVAL IN IRELAND.

> No doubt they rose up early, to observe
> The rite of May; and hearing our intent,
> Came here in grace of our solemnity.
> MIDSUMMER NIGHT'S DREAM.

Remembrances of Old May Day; a Dream of the Past—The Floralia and La Beal-Teine—The Ancient Irish Year—Bael Worship—Ancient Irish Authorities thereon—Bonfires—The May Day Fire in Dublin; a Scene in the Coombe—Bonfire Ceremonial—May Eve Festivities—The Snail Charm and the Yarrow—The Well Ceremonies upon May Morning—Cattle Charms—Nettling—The Hare Witch—Churning—The Butter Witchcraft—May Dew—The May Bush and May Pole—Finglas Sports and Dublin Revels—May Boys and Morris-Dancers—May Rhymes—Saura-Linn—Sonnoughing Sunday—May Day Legends.

WINTER and spring are over; the harsh east winds of March,—the sirocco of the British Isles,—have passed to other climes, and fitful April, now warm and witching, anon rough and gusty, or mild and melting, bright and gloomy, as alternate clouds and sunshine struggle for the mastery—like the face of angry, but forgiving woman, with pouting lip but dimpled cheek, ever smiling through her tears—charming April, the sweet, blue-eyed harbinger of summer, has breathed upon us once again—changing the russet mantle of seed-time into the verdant garment of May. "The middle summer's spring" has come, first budding in mottled green among our sheltered hedges and cultured gardens, then spreading with almost visible pace from shrub to tree, and tree again to lawn; while, as the leaves expand, and young shoots twine as if to screen and shelter from the vulgar gaze the loves of feathered warblers, the birds are mating in every bush, and welcoming the hour with joyous notes of passion or of praise. The summer is bursting upon us. Even the rooks, that balance on the tops of the still grey and unleaved ash, have assumed a softened, cawing note, and the sharp call of the chaffinch assumes a melody in our ears, because we hail it as the season's chime. The timid, retiring primrose, peeps up from among the rib-grass and violets, and raises to the light its modest, sulphur-coloured face; the graceful cowslip, with the crimson star brightening in its calyx, now droops its modest head in the upland, daisy-spangled meadows; and the saucy yellow buttercup and golden Mayflower flaunts it in the deep pastures beside the streamlet's brink, inviting to their honey-cups the bee that now, warmed by the genial season, has shuffled off its lethargy, and is booming over glade and valley. The thorns are putting forth their white clusters, or are already bursting into flower and fragrance, as the sloe, the pear, and the apple are nodding beneath the shower, and strewing the ground with their silvery petals.

Do not our spirits attune with the seasons—springing and expanding with the early summer, but folding up within us as the bleak November blast, cold and cheerless, bursts upon us? Does not the heart gush, the eye brighten, the step become elastic, as we inhale the exhilarating spring breeze in our early country excursions; and again become languid as we seek the summer shade, or bask in the calm repose of autumn? Yes, all nature, marsh and meadow, hill and hollow, land, and sea, and sky, forest monarchs and nodding blue-bell'd florets, beasts and feathered fowls, and winged insects, the tiny myriads of creation—all hail the Sabbath of the year, and sing the matin of the dawn of summer. Let us then, also, hail the season, and for a while throw off the cares of life, as we do the dust of the city, and away to the greenwood shade—there to enjoy the bounteous blessings which nature pours around us; and at the same time revive the recollections of past days and ceremonies, such as our ancestors, simple-hearted, good-natured, superstitious folks, observed of yore upon the bridal of the year.

> "Yes! the summer is returning,
> Warmer, brighter beams are burning;
> Golden mornings, purple evenings,
> Come to glad the world once more.

> Nature, from her long sojourning
> In the winter house of mourning,
> With the light of hope outpeeping,
> From those eyes that late were weeping,
> Cometh dancing o'er the waters,
>   To our distant shore."*

Now then, fair and gentle, rude and rustic readers—country swains and city dames—boys of the Liberty, from Blackpits to Mullinahack, from the banks of the Dodder to the heights of Ballynascorney—girls of Finglas and bucks of Fingal, how have you spent your May Eve?—how did you welcome May Morning, and how do you purpose to celebrate the birth-day of summer? Have you danced to the elfin pipers that played under the thorns of the Phœnix last night? Did you leap through the bonfires that blazed upon Tallaght and Harold's-cross Green? Were you out yester-eve to welcome the " Young May Moon?" or up before sunrise this morning to gather the maiden dew from the sparkling gossamer, to keep the freckles off your pretty faces?—or have you been—

> ———————————— " seeking
> A spell in the young year's flowers.
> The magical May-dew is weeping
> It's charms o'er the summer bow'rs."

Have you found the name of your true love smeared by the snail you set between the plates last evening? and have you chosen a Queen of the May, whose path you'll strew with pasture flowers, as you lead her round the garlanded pole of the Tolka? Are your doors and windows decorated with primroses and cowslips, and May-flowers gathered by the meadows and green inches of your lovely Anna Liffey? Butchers of Patrick's Market and Bull Alley, and boys of the Coombe and the Poddle, are you ready, as of yore, to " cut de bosh, spite of de Devil and de Polis?" Up, weavers of Newmarket and Meath Street, and join with the Ormond boys; will you suffer the white-coated boddaghs of Meath to carry off the prizes at Finglas, and steal the May-dew from the rosy-lipped girls of Glasnevin?

* Mac Carthy's " Bridal of the Year."

Alas! what are we dreaming about—things that were, not are—memories of other, of better and happier times—of ancient customs sneered away by modern utilitarianism—of ceremonies almost forgotten, and healthful rustic sports and pastimes, now prohibited by law, put down by force—starved out of our light-hearted people, or carried beyond the blue waves of the broad Atlantic? Politics have of late years occupied the place of pantomimes—our Finglas sports were interdicted by a special act of the Privy Council—fairy lore has given place to a newspaper political religion—the new police banished the bonfires: and where is the piper or fiddler would enliven the gardens of the "Grinding Young"* after hearing a temperance band, all dressed like Jack Puddings and drum majors coming down the road from Kimmage or Dolphin's Barn?

All gone, dead and gone, save a few dirty urchins in the suburbs, who, with the twigs of a second-hand broom, decked with stinking daffydowndillies, annoy the passengers by asking "a hay'penny to honour the May."

Burgesses and 'prentice boys of Atha-Clea, kings of Dalkey and Mud Island, sweeps of Kevin's Port and the Cabbage Garden,† and coal-porters of Ringsend and Wood Quay, you have either voluntarily surrendered, or been deprived of your ancient sports and pastimes, your festal days, and civic shows. But, "every dog will have his day." Little thought the fat corporators that the hours of the *Fringes*‡ were numbered, and that it would require an I O U from the Lord Mayor to bring out the glass coach on a Candlemas Day.§ Well, have you not had your revenge? The times of Viceregal pageants have passed by; processions, barring a stray funeral up Granby Row, are at an end; Ulster King-at-Arms has become as fabu-

---

* *Grinding Young.* One of the last old Dublin signs, and one of the best executed, too—formerly swinging from a pole, but now nailed to the wall of an almost deserted "public" at Harold's-cross Bridge. In its old *tea-garden* may still be seen several decayed swing-swongs and merry-go-rounds, now too crazy to make the annual excursion to "the Brook"—Donnybrook Fair.

† *Cabbage Garden.* The Capuchin's garden—an old burial ground opposite the Meath Hospital.

‡ *Fringes.* Alluding to the old Corporation custom of Riding the Franchises.

§ Written in April, 1850.

lous a personage as Fin-Ma-Coul, and his tabard and sword have gone with those of the Athlone Herald, to be hung up among the dresses and ornaments of the ancient Celts at the Royal Irish Academy. Guard mountings are mere matters of history; Levees and Drawing-rooms will soon have become stories wherewith to amuse our children, and the shamrock-dressed lady has, perhaps, danced her last in St. Patrick's Hall, and kissed the knocker of Dublin Castle, as she called a sixpenny covered car to carry her home from the wake of our Patron Saint.

Well, happy were the days in Merry England, when blithe King Hal, with Katherine, his Queen, went out a-Maying, and the people walked "into the sweete meadowes and greene woodes, there to rejoice their spirites with the beauty and savour of sweete flowers, and with the harmony of birds"—when royal pageants, with Maid Marians and Morris-dancers, Robin Hoods and Friar Tucks, were considered more wholesome for the people than ale-house polemics; and rustic sports and vil-lage pastimes cheered and solaced the poor man's holiday, and all who met, like Hermia and Lysander of old in the Athenian grove—

> "To do observance to a morn of May."

We sat down, however, to describe Irish, not English sports and ceremonies, and therefore must to our subject at once; for materials abound on every hand upon the May Day customs of the English, and there have been few poets of note in that happy land who have not sung the praises of this blithesome, merry season, when

> "Land and sea
> Give themselves up to jollity;
> And with a heart of May
> Doth every beast keep holiday."

Except in some cursory allusion or incidental notice, May Day in Ireland has not been described by any of the writers with whose works we are familiar. In laying down for our-selves the plan of these popular superstitions of the Irish pea-santry, and the humble classes who are still simple-hearted enough to adhere to the old customs of their forefathers, we originally intended to devote a few chapters to the several festivals, as St. John's Eve, Lady Day, Garland Sunday, St. Martin's Day, Holly Eve, Christmas, Twelfth Night, Candlemas, &c.; and it seems fitting to commence the series with the May festival, May Eve, and May Day, as formerly kept by the Irish, or still, in part, observed by the present generation. But as cows, milk, and butter are supposed to be affected by fairy influences and witchcraft, &c., at that time more particularly than at any other period of the year, we shall now detail so much of the cattle charms from our notes and manuscripts as have immediate reference to the season of the May festival; and reserve for a future period the tales and legends still living in the mouths of the people, and which, better than any description of ours, serve to illustrate the popular opinions as to the causes which produce the various mischances daily occurring to horned cattle, and their produce.

In treating the subject of a festival where a multiplicity and a great variety and diversity of topics must necessarily be introduced, it is not possible to weave it, as in our subsequent chapters, into the form of a tale or legend, expressive of the opinions, as well as descriptive of the phraseology and national character of the people or the scenery of the country.

Many of our May Day customs, sports, and games, are of English origin, and were, no doubt, introduced by the Anglo-Saxons. These pastimes are not, however, confined to the British Isles; many of them are common to all Europe, and several of them have descended to us from the Roman Floralia, or feast of Flora, the goddess of fruits and flowers, which was celebrated of old with great festivity, and sometimes with excessive licentiousness, during the last few days of April and few first of May, when the sun entered the summer solstice. From such customs came down to us the maypoles, and garlands, and floral decorations, the last traditional institution of the summer's welcome; while from our Scandinavian and Celtic great ancestors, we may fairly trace the bonfires—the lucky, or propitiatory, fires which were formerly, and are still in some places, lighted on La-Beal-teine; the Beltin of Scotland, the day of the Beal fire, the Gaelic name by which the period is still called.

The English ceremonial of May Day has been fully and graphically described by the industrious Brande, and by Sir Henry Ellis, in his modern edition of the work of that author, in Hone's "Every-day Book," in Strutt's "Sports and Pastimes of the People," and in several minor works and periodicals. But in describing the Irish observances of this institution, we shall only make use of these and other authorities where they serve to illustrate, by their more ample details, our now almost forgotten Irish customs. It is scarcely necessary to inform the reader that a superstitious creed, and certain mystic rites derived from the remotest times, attach to almost every nation in a certain state of society, and are not peculiar to either race or creed; that some of these are of almost universal acceptation; that others belong to peculiar localities, and that their geographical distribution is a source of interesting investigation both to the historian and to the ethnologist. In many countries these rites and practices are still prevalent; in others more advanced in civilization, or the society of which has suffered some sudden and violent disruption, they are merely preserved in the ancient ballad, the bardic legend, or the traditional romance; or dimly appear referred to in the sayings and proverbs of the old people, or have been preserved like lingering shadows amongst the amusements and customs of modern times. In describing any peculiar rite or custom, we shall give it in as full and ample a manner as we have ever heard or known it to be observed or enacted. But as many of these usages are now obsolete, others only partially preserved—some being very local, one custom being confined to the north, another being peculiar to the west, and several only seen in the south, or in the adjacent parts of Leinster—our country readers are not to suppose that, because only a mere vestige of the rite or type of the ceremonial exists in their neighbourhood, we have in any way enlarged these descriptions by fancy or conjecture.

This little work is not intended for antiquarian purposes. We have neither the leisure nor the research necessary to render it learned in an archæological point of view, but it is our earnest desire, as far as our knowledge enables us, not to propagate, even in a popular legend, the usual historic fallacies, conjectural etymologies, and far-fetched and often inapplicable and unmeaning analogies to Egyptian, Hindoo, and Persian mythologies—high sounding names often used to cloak the ignorance of writers or to mystify the simplicity and credulity of readers,—which obtained credit with Irish readers some years ago; and it is our wish, as far as possible, to correct those opinions which the simplicity or ignorance of our forefathers disseminated.

It is more than probable that the ancient pagan Irish worshipped the Sun, but whether under the name of *Beal*, or with what symbolic idols, is as yet undetermined; we also know that the first great division of the year* was into summer and winter, *Samradh* and *Geimhredh;* the former beginning in May, or *Bealtine;* and the latter in November, or *Samhfhuim*, Summer-end. Now most credible authorities are agreed that the first great Druid feast, or fire-offering of Beal, *Bel* or *Baal*, was originally kept on the first of May, though afterwards altered, it is said, by the early Christian missionaries† to midsummer, when it celebrates the Eve of St. John the Baptist's Day (the 24th of June), under which head we purpose describing this very ancient pagan custom, with all the Irish rites attending it more particularly on another occasion. But we have still stronger proof than either that derived from learned writings, or the very name itself, in the fact that bonfires are still lighted in some places in Ireland on the last evening in April, and in others on the 1st of May. We have seen them but a very few years ago in the county of Wicklow, and in the neighbourhood of Dublin, and several used to be lighted in the

---

* See "O'Donovan's Introduction to the *Laebhar na g-Ceart*, or Book of Rights," published by the Irish Celtic Society, "On the Division of the Year among the Ancient Irish," p. xlviii. Other divisions into quarters, or *ratha*, as *Samh-ratha, Foghmhar-ratha, Geimh-ratha*, and *Iar-ratha*, or *Earrach*, corresponding to our summer, autumn, winter, and spring (see Dr. O'Conor's "Rerum Hib. Scrip. Epistola Nuncupatoria," lxxi.) were also made; but these do not concern our present purpose.

† We do not know when this actually occurred, or through whose instrumentality. The country people attribute it to St. Patrick, but we know not from what source. Can any of our readers enlighten us upon this point. Do the Bollandists allude to it?

back streets and lanes, particularly in the Liberties of this city, until the establishment of the present admirable police force. Vallancey—whose opinions, though deserving of little weight, when questions of history or the discussion of theories relative to antiquities and etymologies are concerned, is fully worthy of credence when mere matters of fact, or circumstances passing beneath his own knowledge, are under review—says speaking of the Scottish Beltin :—" The Irish still preserve this custom, for the fire is to this day lighted in the milking yards; the men, women, and children, for the same reason, pass through, or leap over, the sacred fires, and the cattle are driven through the flames of the burning straw on the 1st of May."* A correspondent to " Hone's Every-day Book" (vol. ii., p. 595) thus describes the Dublin bonfire so late as 1825. A portion of the collection made by the May-boys was " expended in the purchase of a heap of turf sufficient for a large fire, and, if the funds would allow, an old tar-barrel. Formerly it was not considered complete without having a horse's skull and other bones to burn in the fire. The depots for these bones were the tanners' yards, in a part of the suburbs called Kilmainham,† and on May morning groups of boys dragged loads of bones to their several destinations." This practice has given rise to the threat still made use of, " I will drag you like a horse's head to a bonfire." The great Dublin bonfire, which used in former times to blaze in the open space leading from St. Patrick's Cathedral to the Coombe, upon May Eve, is still within the recollection of the old inhabitants. And up to this very time the May-bush in the neighbourhood of Swords and other places is, at dusk, decorated with a number of lighted candles, like the *Heilege-nacht-Baum*, the good, or holy, or lucky tree of Christmas in Germany. May bonfires are not common in Connaught or Ulster, but they still maintain in Cork, and in parts of Kilkenny, Limerick and Kerry. Now, it is remarkable that while the May bonfires are always lighted upon the evening of the 30th

* See Vallancey's " Enquiry into the First Inhabitants of Ireland," vol. ii. of the " Collectanea de Rebus Hibernicis," p. 64.

† There are but few tan-yards in this or any other part of Dublin now, and the value of bones is too well known at present to permit of their ever being used for mere matter of amusement.

of April or the 1st of May, the midsummer fire is, in many places, repeated twelve days after the 21st of June, that period marking the difference between the Old and New Style, a fact which goes a good way to prove that the institution of the midsummer fire is of comparatively modern date. The 29th of June—St. Peter and St. Paul's Day—has also of late years been in some places honoured with a bonfire; so that soon the people will have altogether forgotten the original institution of the bonfire, and, perhaps, have given it up altogether. Some old persons, still alive, tell us of the cattle having been driven through the half-extinguished bonfire, as a preservative against witchcraft, and people used to leap through it, and carry off a coal from it, as at the fire of St. John's Eve; and the ceremonial observed in Scotland, up to a very recent date indeed, of which accounts have been preserved by Campbell * and others, afford us ample food for speculation and conjecture (even had we no Irish authorities to consult) as to the pagan rites originally enacted at this festival, which, it would appear, in times of remote antiquity, evidently partook of the nature of a sacrifice, or propitiatory offering to the sun.

Mr. W. Grant Stewart, in his "Popular Superstitions and Festive Amusements of the Highlands of Scotland," (1823), has given an account of several curious rites performed even in modern days in that country. "At Belton Eve," he says, " messengers are dispatched to the woods for cargoes of the blessed rowan-tree, the virtues of which are well known. Being formed into the shape of a cross, by means of a red-thread, the virtues of which, too, are very eminent, those crosses are, with all due solemnity, inserted in the different door-lintels in the town, and protect those premises from the cantrips of the most diabolical witch in the universe. Care should also be taken to insert one of them in the midden, which has at all times been a favourite site of *rendezvous* with the black sisterhood. This cheaply-purchased precaution once observed, the people of those

* See " Journey to Edinburgh." Consult, also, Dalzell's " Darker Superstitions of Scotland," pp. 167 and 177. George Cruikshank has given a graphic illustration of the May-dew dancers at Arthur's Seat, Edinburgh, in " Hone's Every-day Book," vol. ii., p. 610. See also Martin's Description of the Western Islands of Scotland p. 7.

countries will now go to bed as unconcernedly, and sleep as soundly, as on any other night.

"While those necessary precautions are in preparation, the matron or housekeeper is employed in a not less interesting avocation to the juvenile generation, *i. e.*, baking the Belton bannocks. Next morning the children are presented each with a bannock, with as much joy as an heir to an estate his title-deeds; and having their pockets well lined with cheese and eggs, to render the entertainment still more sumptuous, they hasten to the place of assignation, to meet the little band assembled on the brow of some sloping hill, to reel their bannocks and learn their future fate. With hearty greetings they meet, and with their knives make the signs of life and death on their bannocks. These signs are a cross, or the sign of life, on the one side; and a cypher, or the sign of death, on the other. This being done, the bannocks are all arranged in a line, and on their edges let down the hill. This process is repeated three times, and if the cross most frequently present itself, the owner will live to celebrate another Belton day; but if the cypher is oftenest uppermost, he is doomed to die, of course. This sure prophecy of short life, however, seldom spoils the appetites of the unfortunate short-livers, who will handle their knives with as little sign of death as their more fortunate companions. Assembling around a rousing fire of collected heath and brush-wood, the ill-fated bannocks are soon demolished, amidst the cheering and jollity of the youthful association."

The Gaelic appellation *Bealtaine*, the *Beal-fire*, has given rise to many conjectures, and would, at first sight, appear to be strongly corroborative of the Syrian or Phœnician origin of the Irish, from the circumstance of the name of the chief deity of the two nations being the same, and from the fact of fire being considered propitiatory in both countries. It remains, however, to be proved that the Irish had a god called Baal or Beal, unless it can be shown that they worshipped the sun under that title or name. It is asserted that if the Pagan Irish worshipped Baal, there would be more places called so in ancient topographical descriptions, or preserved in modern names; but it is not so. Thus, to our inquiry on this head, Mr.

O'Donovan writes:—"There are no places called *Baal* in Ireland. I met some places called *Bealtaine*, from May-fires having been lighted there. The *Balls* in Achill Island, in the county of Mayo, are portions of land allotted to individuals, as Conor Patten's *Ball*, Denis Toland's *Ball*, &c. In this sense, the word ʙᴀʟʟ denotes a ꜱᴘᴏᴛ (of land). *Ball*, the village in Mayo, is from ʙᴀʟʟᴀ, a *wall*. The *Ballys* are from ᴃᴀɪʟᴇ, Villa, πολις, *ville* ; and the *Bellas*, from *Bel-atha*, *i. e.*, mouth of a ford, *os vadi*." But it may be said, on the other hand, that there are not places called after any other Irish Pagan deities either.

The references to the Belteine period are scarce in the Irish annals. In "The Restrictions and Prerogatives of the Kings of Eire," given in the recently published "Book of Rights," to the learned introduction to which we referred in a previous note (p. 38), all the authorities are cited. In the text of that work we read that the monarch was not "to go in a ship upon the water the Monday after Bealltaine (May Day)." Again, in the poetic description, we find, among the restrictions of the Ultonian monarch, that he was not "to bathe on May Day eastwards in the bright and beautiful Loch Feabhail;" probably from some such superstititious fear like that which the present inhabitants of England, as well as Ireland have with respect to going near water on Whit Monday.

In an ancient Irish manuscript, in Trinity College Library, we find this reference to the Summer-Advent fire :—

" *Beltine, i.e., Biltine, i.e.*, lucky fire (bon-fire), *i.e.*, two fires which used to be made by the lawgivers, or Druids, with great incantations, and they used to drive the cattle between them (to guard) against the diseases of each year. Or Bel-dine: Bel was the name of an idol god. It was on it (*i.e.*, that day) that the firstlings of every kind of cattle used to be exhibited as in the possession of Bel ; *vide* Beldine."*

In " Cormac's Glossary," we read the following explanation of Bealtaine, as well as the form of purification of the cattle, which was observed at this great Pagan ceremonial :—

* See Dr. Petrie's learned "Essay on Tara," p. 84; and Professor O'Donovan's "Introduction to the Book of Rights," p. 43.

"*Belltaine, i.e., Bill-tene, i.e.,* tene-bil, *i.e.,* goodly fire (bon, or bonus fire), *i.e.,* two lucky fires the Druids used to make with great incantations over them, and they used to drive the cattle between them (to preserve them) against the diseases of each year."

In another part of the "Glossary," however, Cormac explains *Bel* as an *idol* or *false god.*

Keating has the following notice of the fire lighted at Uisneach, close to Ballymore, in Westmeath, in the reign of Tuathal Teachtmhar :—

"He (Tuathal) erected the second palace in that part of Meath which was taken from Connaught, viz., at Uisneach, where was held a general meeting of the men of Erin, called the meeting of Uisneach. This fair, or assembly, was held on the first day of the month of May; and they were wont to exchange and barter their cattle, jewels, and other property there. They were also accustomed to make offerings to the chief god which they worshipped, named *Bel;* and it was a custom with them to make *two fires* in honour of this Bel in every cantred of Ireland, and to drive a couple of every kind of cattle in the cantred between the two fires, as a preservation, to protect them against every disease during that year. And it was from this fire, made in honour of *Bel,* that the noble festival of Phillip and James (*i.e.,* the 1st of May) is called *Beilteine, i.e.,* the fire of *Bel.*"

"I never could discover," writes Mr. O'Donovan, in answer to a query of ours on the subject, "where Keating found authority for lighting this fire at Uisneach; and I have been long of opinion that this fire was lighted at Tlachtgha, a hill near Athboy, in East Meath, where the same King Tuathal is said to have erected another palace. I ground this opinion upon a passage in a MS. in the library of Trinity College, Dublin, which runs thus :—

"The fair of Tlachtgha (which belongs to that part of Meath taken from the province of Munster) was celebrated by the youths of Munster; and a fire was lighted thereat, from which all the fires lighted in Erin were kindled, which were purchased from them (the youths of Munster); and a *screpall* of gold was paid them out of every territory in Erin for the fire, and a sack of wheat, and a hog from every chief hearth in Erin, were given to the Comharba of Meath, *i.e.*, O'Kindellan, for this fire."— H. 3, 17, p. 732.

Bon, not bone-fires (ᴄeıne ᴄnáṁaᴄ), are evidently synonymous, if not identical, with Beal-fires; but if Bel, Belus, or Beal, was really a god worshipped here, there is no reason why the name of the festival and the rite should not have been derived from his name; but except in Keating, and the hint in Cormac Mac Cullinan's Dictionary, there are, we understand, no other Irish authorities for it. The virtues of fire as a disinfectant of the atmosphere, and a preventive to the spread of contagious diseases, is a very popular and widely-spread belief among the Irish peasantry; and it is remarkable that, on the first approach of cholera here, in 1831, a sacred purifying fire —by some wise heads supposed to be of a political nature— went the round of the island, under the name of The Blessed Turf. It was carried from house to house with such rapidity, that it traversed the whole island in a single night. A remnant of the people still believe in the efficacy of fire as a preservative against pestilence, and sew up a piece of charmed turf in their dress for that purpose.

In early scripture history, we read that the people not only passed their cattle, but their children, through the idolatrous fires of Baal and Moloch. In that most charming work, " Martin's Description of the Western Islands of Scotland," (1703), which is, perhaps, the best account extant of the superstitions, manners, customs, and popular opinions of the Celtic people, we have the following account of *La Bealtaine* in the Hebrides :—

" Another god of the Britains was Belus, or Belinus, which seems to have been the Assyrian god Bel or Belus; and, probably, from this pagan deity comes the Scots' term of Beltin, the first day of May, having its first rise from the custom practised by the Druids, in the isles, of extinguishing all the fires in the parish until the tithes were paid; and upon payment of them, the fires were kindled in each family, and never till then. In those days malefactors were burnt between two fires; hence, when they would express a man to be in a great strait, they say, 'He is between two fires of Bell.'"   And again, in another place, he says, "The inhabitants here did also make use of a fire called Tin-Egin, *i.e.*, a forced fire, or fire of necessity, which they used as an antidote against the plague, or murrain, in cattle; and it was performed thus: all the fires in the parish were extinguished, and then eighty-one married men, being thought the necessary number for effecting this design, took two great planks of wood, and nine of them were employed by turns, who, by their repeated efforts, rubbed one of the planks against the other until the heat thereof produced fire; and from this forced fire each family is supplied with new fire, which is no sooner kindled, than a potful of water is quickly set on it, and afterwards sprinkled upon the people infected with the plague, or upon the cattle that have the murrain, and this they all say they find successful by experience.   It was practised in the main land opposite to the South of Skie, within these thirty years."

There is but one other inquiry connected with *Bealtaine,* which here claims our notice.   The ingenious and learned Dr. O'Conor, of Ballinagar, supposed that the fire which was lighted on Tara Hill, by the Druids of King Laeghaire, upon the night of St. Patrick's encampment at Slane, was the Bealtaine, or Fire-Feast of *Samhrath ;* but if the earliest and most authentic biographers of Patrick are to be credited, that night was Easter-eve, or Holy Saturday, the 21st March, A.D. 433, and not May Day; and the Stowe librarian has not, it appears, sustained his position by arguments sufficient to convince our modern investigators, Dr. Petrie and Professor O'Donovan, the latter of whom writes :—" The probability then is, that the fire lighted at Teamhair on Easter Eve, A.D. 433, was not the *Bealtaine*, but some other fire; and it is stated in the second life of St. Patrick, published by Colgan, that it was the Feis Teamhrach, or Feast of Teamhrach, that Laeghaire and his Satraps were celebrating on the occasion; while the author of the Life of St. Patrick, in the 'Book of Lismore,' asserts that Laeghaire was then celebrating the festival of his own nativity, which appears to have been the truth; and if so, it was not the regular septennial Feis which met after Samhain, but one convened to celebrate the king's birthday. From these notices, it is quite clear that O'Conor's inference, that the *Bealtaine* was lighted on the 21st of March, by the pagan Irish, is not sustained. In the accounts given of the *Bealtaine*, in 'Cormack's Glossary,' and in H. 3, 18, p. 596, as quoted in 'Petrie's Antiquities of Tara Hill,' *no time is specified* for the lighting of it, nor could we be able from them, or from any other written evidence yet discovered, to decide at what season it was lighted, were it not that the first of May is still universally called in Irish *La Bealtaine*. But Dr. O'Conor argues that this name was applied in pagan times to the 21st of March, and that it was transferred to the 1st of May by the early Christians, to agree with a Christian festival. This, however, is contrary to the tradition which still prevails in many parts of Ireland, namely, that the fires lighted in pagan times, on the 1st of May, were transferred by St. Patrick to the 24th of June, in honour of St. John the Baptist, on the eve of whose festival they still light bonfires in every county in Ireland."*

Many ancient ceremonies, as well as bonfires, attached to Midsummer Eve in England, up to a comparatively recent period; but, with the exception of the rites performed in connexion with the fire itself, we know of no Irish usages peculiar to the Christian festival of St. John's Eve; while numberless were the ancient customs observed either on the vigil of the summer quarter, or on May Day, in Ireland, vestiges of which still linger among the people—facts strongly corroborative of the supposition that the Midsummer fire is but the ingrafting of an ancient *pagan* rite upon a comparatively modern *Christian* festival. Let those who daily boast of adult conversions from one creed to another look well to the fact, that notwithstanding all the efforts of a most powerful Church, and all the influence of the Irish clergy, of every denomination, the May Day bonfire, the pagan fire which Cormac Cullinan told us was lighted in honour of the god Bel, in his time, still exists in many parts of

* O'Donovan's "Introduction to the Leabhar na g-Ceart," p. 50. See also Petrie's "Essay upon Tara," in the Transactions of the Royal Irish Academy, p. 84.

the country, and still lingers in the remembrance of all our old people, now after fourteen hundred years of so-called conversion to Christianity.

We might reserve the details of the Midsummer fire until we came to describe that festival more particularly; but any account of the ceremonial attending the fire lighted upon St. John's Eve is much more applicable to the May fire; and much of the ceremonial of the former is still retained wherever the *Bealtaine* is even partially observed. The preparations for the May Day sports and ceremonial in Dublin, commenced about the middle of April, and even earlier, and a rivalry, which often led to the most fearful riots was incited, particularly between the "Liberty boys" upon the south, and the "Ormond boys" upon the north side of the river; and even among themselves, as to which street or district would exhibit the best dressed and handsomest May bush, or could boast the largest and hottest bonfire. Upon one of the popular outbreaks resulting from the abduction of a May bush, was written the song, in old Dublin slang, of—

"De nite afore de fust of Magay,"

so spiritedly described in that graphic record of the past, "Sketches of Ireland Sixty Years Ago," now republished as a part of this series. For weeks before, a parcel of idle scamps, male and female, devoted themselves to the task of "collecting for the May;" and parties, decorated with ribbons, and carrying green boughs, and sometimes escorted by itinerant musicians, went from house to house soliciting contributions of ribbons, handkerchiefs, and pieces of gaudy silk—materials then manufactured, and consequently more common in the Liberty than now—to adorn the May bush. Turf, coals, old bones, particularly *slugs* of cows' horns from the tan-yards, and horses' heads from the knackers, logs of wood, &c., were also collected, to which some of the merchants generally added a few pitch and tar-barrels. Money was solicited to "moisten the clay" of the revellers; for, whether from liking, or from fear, or considering it unlucky, few ventured to refuse to contribute "something toste de May bush." The ignitable materials were formed in depots, in back-yards, and the cellars of old houses, long before the approaching festival; and several *sorties* were made by opposing factions to gain possession of these hordes, and lives have been lost in the skirmishes which ensued. In Dublin the bonfires were always lighted upon the evening of May Day, and generally in the vicinity of the May bush. The great fire was, as we already mentioned, at the lower end of the Coombe; but there were also fires in the centre and at the top of that classic locality. The weavers had their fire in Weaver's Square; the hatters and pipemakers in the upper end of James's Street; and the neighbourhood of St. John's Well, near Kilmainham, beside Bully's Acre, generally exhibited a towering blaze. Upon the north side of the city, the best fire blazed in Smithfield. With the exception of one ancient rite —that of throwing into it the May bush—there were but few Pagan ceremonies observed at the metropolitan fires. A vast crowd collected, whiskey was distributed *galore* both to those who had, and had not, gathered the morning's dew. The entire population of the district collected round the bush and the fire; the elder portion, men and women, bringing with them chairs or stools, to sit out the wake of the winter and spring, according to the olden usage. The best singers in the crowd lilted up, "The Night before Larry was Stretched," or "Hie for de Sweet Libertie;" but the then popular air of "The Baiting of Lord Altham's Bull," and "De May bush;" and another local song of triumphful commemoration of a victory over the Ormond-market men, a verse of which we remember:—

> " Begone, ye cowardly scoundrels,
> Do ye remember de day,
> Dat yes came down to Newmarket,
> And stole de sweet May bush away?"

were the "most popular and deservedly admired," from their allusions to the season and the locality. Fiddlers and pipers plied their fingers and elbows; and dancing, shouting, revelry, and debauchery of every description succeeded, till, at an advanced hour of the night, the scene partook more of the nature of the ancient Saturnalia, than anything we can at present liken it to, except that which a London mob *now* exhibits the

night preceding an execution in the Old Bailey or at Horse-
monger Lane Gaol.

In country parts, however, besides the ordinary expressions
of delight, generated by the amusement of the bonfire, the an-
cient Druidical custom of leaping through the flames, was prac-
tised at May as well as upon Midsummer Eve, as of old at the
Roman Palilia—

> " Moxque per ardentes stipulæ crepitantis acervos,
>   Tiajicias celeri strenua membra pede."

With some, particularly the younger portion, this was a
mere diversion, to which they attached no particular meaning.
Yet others performed it with a deeper intention, and evidently
as a religious rite.   Thus, many of the old people might be seen
circumambulating the fire, and repeating to themselves certain
prayers.   If a man was about to perform a long journey, he
leaped backwards and forwards three times through the fire, to
give him success in his undertaking.   If about to wed he did it
to purify himself for the marriage state.   If going to under-
take some hazardous enterprise, he passed through the fire
to render himself invulnerable.   As the fire sunk low, the girls
tript across it to procure good husbands ; women great with
child might be seen stepping through it to ensure a happy
delivery, and children were also carried across the smouldering
ashes, as of old among the Canaanites. When the fire has nearly
expired, and the dancing, singing, and carousing are over, each
individual present provides himself with a *braune*, or ember of
the fire, to carry home with him, which, if it becomes extin-
guished before he reaches his house, it is an omen of impending
misfortune.   The new fire is kindled with this spark.   They
also throw some of these lighted coals, or ashes, into the corn-
fields, or among the potato crops, or the flax, to preserve them
from witchcraft, and to ensure a good return.   Portions of the
extinguished fire are generally retained in each family, and
often sewed into the dress of an individual about to cross the
sea.*   Hecker, in his description of the Epidemics of the

* In addition to the references and quotations given in the foregoing notices
of *Bealtaine*, the following works may be consulted :—Wood's " Inquiry concern-
ing the Primitive Inhabitants of Ireland," p. 170; " The Penny Magazine ;"
" Notices of May Day and Midsummer ;" " The Philosophical Survey of the

Middle Ages, relates many curious usages formerly resorted to upon the kindling of the " Nadfyr " on St. John's Day (when the dancing mania first commenced in Germany), which are equally applicable to the May festival.

As at the Midsummer festival so at the May fires, the boys of an adjoining bonfire often made a sudden descent, and endeavoured to carry off some of the fuel from a neighbouring bonfire, and serious consequences have resulted therefrom. When all was over, it was no uncommon practice, in Connaught at least, at the Midsummer fire, to drive the cattle through the *greeshagh*, or warm ashes, as a form of purification and a preservative against witchcraft, fairies, murrain, blackleg, loss of milk, and other misfortunes or diseases. Even the ashes which remain bear a charm or virtue, and were sprinkled about like the red and yellow powders at the Hindoo festival of *Hoolie*. In former times some used to be collected and mixed with water; and this liquor, after some days, when the ashes had precipitated, was poured off, and used as a wash for sores of different descriptions. To this day the annual, or half-yearly rent paid by the farmers in the south of Ireland in May, is called *Cios na Bealtaine*, or the rent of Baal's fire.

Do not the following lines from Barnabe Googe's translation of Neogeorgus' quaint old poem,* descriptive of the Midsummer

South of Ireland," p. 233; Crantz' "History of Greenland," Vol. II.; "The Mount of Dromore," in Stott's "Songs of Dearded;" Moore's "History of Ireland" (Cab. Cyclo.), Vol. I, pp. 22, 24, 205, 216; "Transactions of Royal Irish Academy," Vol. I., Antiq. pp. 4 and 7; Vol. II., p. 78, giving an account of the "Hobby Horse," now obsolete; Vol. XX.; Petrie's "Round Towers;" Croker's "Researches in the South of Ireland;" Train's "Historical and Statistical Account of the Isle of Man;" Sir Wm. Betham's "Gael and Cimbri," p. 222; Vallancey's "Collectanea," Vol. II., p. 286; Duffy's "Irish Catholic Magazine;" Vol. I., p. 12, &c. In the "Dublin University Magazine," for Oct. 1849, see "Song of the Ramoan Peasantry on May Eve;" Betham's "Etruria Celtica;" Pennant's "Tour in Scotland, 1769," p. 110; "The Newry Magazine;" O'Halloran's "History of Ireland;" "Rees' Cyclopædia," Art. *Beltine;* Borlase, p. 134; Higgins's "Celtic Druids," p. 150; "Archæologia," Vol. VII., p. 102, X., 181; Toland's "Druids;" Campbell's "Ireland." See also the German works of Grim. The discussion of the opinions of these various authors, or even an enumeration of the subjects relating to May Day customs contained in their works, would occupy more space than we could here devote to this matter.

* Translated in 1750, and dedicated to Queen Elizabeth. See Brand's "Popular Antiquities," and Strutt's "Sports and Pastimes."

Eve festival, appear to describe some of our May Day rites, particularly that of looking through the flower-decorated bush into the bonfire :—

" When bonfires great with loftie flame in every towne doe burne,
  And young men round about with maides doe dance in every streete,
  With garlands wrought of mother-wort, or else with virvaine sweete,
  And many other flowres faire, with violets in their handes ;
  Whereas they all doe fondly thinke that whosoever standes,
  And, throw the flowres, beholdes the flame, his eyes shall feel no paine;
  When thus till night they daunced have, they through the fire amaine
  With stormy wordes doe runne, and all their hearbes they cast therein,
  And then with words devout and prayers they solemnly begin,
  Desiring God that all their ills may there consumed bee,
  Whereby they thinke through all that yeare from agues to be free."

We have never heard of any floral accompaniments to the St. John's Eve fire in Ireland.

Cattle are carefully watched about May time, but particularly upon May Eve and May Day. In the South and West they are invariably housed or confined in an inclosed paddock, and carefully watched during the night, particularly milch cows, calves, and heifers; for, if any one was to milk three titfuls in the name of the devil, or even go through the form of milking the spancel, or *langling*, as it is called in some of the counties of Leinster, there would be but a Flemish account of the butter for the next twelvemonth.

The *Nech-na Bealltaine*, or May Eve, has been from time immemorial a season of rejoicing and festivity, although we are not aware of any games or pastimes peculiar to it; but the advent of the first day of summer is always hailed with delight by the peasantry, who then meet in the evening upon village-greens, or at cross-roads, and such other assembling places of the people. The May bush, though seldom decorated, was always erected then; and, if the weather was fine, dancing and music gladdened the hearts of the old crones and shanaghies that gathered round the neighbouring doors, or leaned against the adjoining ditches, and compared the present with the former times, when they, too, could *fut it* to " Morgan Ratler " or " Planxty Conor," or listen to the Irish song of " Summer is coming." If there is any one scene in the Irish peasant's life which approaches the description of the dance given in Goldsmith's " Deserted Village," it is that observed upon May Eve. At this time, also, small-plays and various rural games are resorted to, as " dance in the ring," and " threading my grandmother's needle;" in which latter the boys and the girls join hands and dance a sort of serpentine figure up and down the roads, sometimes for a mile in extent *—the men generally carrying green boughs, or sprigs of sloe and white-thorn, then in blossom, and the girls decked with *posies*, wreaths of *noneens* (daisies), and garlands of May-flowers and buttercups.

As the evening advances, and the assembly breaks up into small parties, lovers seeking the greenwood shade, and crones retiring to the hob, a few solitary individuals may be seen walking out in the gloaming, courting the moonlight by the ancient rath, or wandering into the lone fairy-peopled valley, or the dreary fell, in hopes of hearing the mystic pipers of the *sheogues*, which on that night, more than any other, are said to be on the alert, and to favour mortals with their melodies. Great is the agility and grace believed to be conferred on those who are fortunate enough to trip it to the music of the fairy pipes; so great that it has become a proverb in Connaught, upon seeing a good dancer, to say, " Troth, *ma bouchel*, you listened to the piper on May Eve."

The hearth is always carefully swept on May Eve, and then lightly sprinkled over with some of the turf-ashes; if, in the morning, the print of a foot is seen on it pointing towards the door, it is fully expected that some one will die before that day twelvemonth.

The snail charm, described by Gay in the " Shepherd's Week," though probably of English extraction, is even yet very general in Ireland, but is chiefly performed by the girls. The

* For a particular account of this dance, see the third chapter of " Jenny Ramsay," lately published by Mr. Francis Davis, in the " Belfast Man's Journal" for January 26th, 1850. To the talented and enthusiastic author and editor of that work, we are much indebted for valuable information upon the northern superstitions. We have seen this dance performed on the Arœopagus of Athens by the Greeks upon Easter Sunday. Dancing in a circle and performing other similar evolutions, like the *Le Bal* of the people of Brittany, though resorted to merely as an amusement now, is evidently the relic of the ancient mystic dance of Druidism.

little animal pressed into the service on this occasion is not the box-snail (or *shellemidah*), but what is commonly called the *Druthsen*, or slug, and should be discovered accidentally, not sought for; when found, it is either placed between two pewter plates, or upon a table previously sprinkled with ashes or flour, and covered with a *mias*, or wooden bowl; and in the morning the anxious maid seeks to discover in the slimy track left by the snail's nocturnal peregrinations, the initial of her secret lover's name :—

> " Slow crawl'd the snail, and if I right can spell,
> In the soft ashes marked a curious L ;
> Oh, may the wondrous omen lucky prove !
> For L is found in Lubberkin and Love."*

In the North, particularly in Raherty Island, several May Day superstitions, resembling those usually performed at Hollandtide, still remain. If a young woman wishes to know who is to be her future spouse, she goes, late on May Eve, to a black sally-tree, and plucks therefrom nine sprigs, the last of which she throws over her right shoulder, and puts the remaining eight into the foot of her right stocking. She then, on her knees, reads the third verse of the 17th chapter of Job; and on going to bed she places the stocking, with its contents, under her head. These rites duly performed, and her faith being strong, she will, in a dream during the night, be treated to a sight of her future husband.

Another mode of obtaining the same knowledge consists in going, after sunset on May Eve, to a bank on which the yarrow (*ahirhallunc*) is growing plentifully, and gathering therefrom nine sprigs of the plant, while she repeats the following words :—

> " Good morrow, good morrow, fair yarrow ;
> And thrice good morrow to thee ;
> Come tell me before to-morrow
> Who my true love shall be."

The yarrow is brought home, put into the right-foot stocking, placed under the pillow, and the mystic dream is confidently

* Were the snails so employed under mesmeric influence, like those lately described by a learned Scotch professor?

expected. But if the girl opens her lips to speak after she has pulled the yarrow, the charm is broken.

In another mode of consulting the oracle of love, often resorted to in the South, the maiden seeks a neighbouring well and dropping a noggin into it, while she repeats the name of the object of her affection, leaves it there for the night, but returns to the spot by daybreak next morning. Should the vessel be found floating on the surface, she may fairly hope for the consummation of her heart's ambition; but if it has sunk she despairs of such a happiness, "for that offer, anyhow."

Wells, whether blessed by saint, or consecrated by pilgrim's "rounds," or merely furnishing the healthful spring, are objects of especial care and attention at May time; and, in former years, were frequently watched all night, particularly in pastoral districts, to ensure them against being "skimmed" with a wooden dish, or *cuppaun*, by some butter-abducting hag, as the sun rose on May morning. This was called "taking the flower of the well;" and the words, "Come butter, come," were then repeated.

Farmers drive their flocks by daybreak to the wells, that they may drink there before those of their neighbours, and the greatest rivalry prevails amongst the servant-girls and milk-maids, as to who should first draw water from the spring-well upon May morning.

When potatoes were plenty, and before Free Trade had smashed the cattle-feeding small farmer, it was customary for every member of the family to go out to these well-gatherings for syllabubs early in the morning, each with a small vessel in his hand, containing a drop of whiskey, on which the cow was milked; but cattle and farmer, whiskey and noggin, servants and all—are gone.

"My grandfather," writes one of our correspondents, "once came upon an old woman mixing a small piece of what appeared to be butter, on a May morning, and muttering strange words over it. She was sticking it against the door of a cow-house; and when she found that he perceived her, she suddenly fled, leaving the piece of butter behind, stuck like putty to the jamb of the door. He took it home, and found it to be not butter, but a mixture of flour and other things, which he believed was intended by her as a charm. He also caught an old woman, on a May-morning, at a spring well, cutting the tops of water-cresses with a pair of scissors, muttering strange words, and the names of certain persons who had cows; and also the words, *is liom-sa leaċ do ċoda-sa,*—*i.e. half thine is mine.* She repeated these words as often as she cut a sprig of water-cress with the scissors, which sprig personated the individual whom she intended to rob of his milk and butter. After listening to her for some time he rushed from his place of concealment, and making towards the well, cried out, *is liom-sa leaċ do ċoda-sa;* but the affrighted *cailleach* fled, leaving behind a lump of butter, a *baurach*, or cow spancel, and other things which I now forget."

On no account would either fire or water—but, above all things, a coal of fire, even the kindling of a pipe—be given, for love or money, out of a house during the entire of May Day. The piece of lighted turf used to kindle another fire is styled the *seed* of the fire; and this people endeavoured to procure from the bonfire of the previous night, and to keep it alive in the ashes to light the fire on May morning; but a large fire should not be " made down " early on May morning, as it is believed that witches and fairies, whom they desire to propitiate, have great horror to the first smoke.

Milch cows, heifers, and calves, are the objects of peculiar care at May time, from the very popular and widely-spread belief in their being then, more than at any other time, susceptible of evil influences, and when not housed early upon May Eve, are driven into an inclosed paddock, the four corners of which, as well as the cattle themselves, used in former times to be sprinkled with holy water, and in some places, every angle of the land, and every four-footed beast belonging to the farm was subject to the like purifying process, particularly with the water blessed upon Easter Sunday. The more superstitious among the people, and those who adhered to the remnants of the Pagan customs of their Celtic ancestors, put a *soogaun* of! straw round the neck of each cow upon May Eve, in order to preserve it from ill luck or the *good people ;* and should the cattle be kept in a confined yard or field, every precaution was taken to prevent their breaking the bounds of their inclosure during the night. We have known each head of cattle to be slightly singed with lighted straw upon May Eve, or to have a lighted coal passed round their bodies, as is customary after calving; and it was not unusual, some fifteen or twenty years ago, to bleed a whole herd of cattle upon a May morning, and then to dry and burn the blood. We have more than once, when a boy, seen the entire of the great Fort of Rathcroghan, then the centre of one of the most extensive and fertile grazing districts of Connaught, literally reddened with the blood thus drawn upon a May morning. Bleeding the cattle at this period of the year was evidently done with a sanitary intention, as some of the older medical works recommended in the human subject; but choosing that particular day, and subsequently burning the blood, were evidently the vestiges of some Heathen rite. In some districts, and particularly during hard times, some of the blood thus drawn used to be mixed with meal, boiled into a posset, and eaten by the herds and the poor people. But many of these ceremonies, having been either laughed at or positively interdicted by the more educated Roman Catholic clergy, are fast falling into disuse. Not only is it considered unlucky to permit fire to be removed from the house until after the meridian at least, but many people would not give away, even in charity, a drop of milk, or a bit of bread or butter, on May Day, or lend churn, churndash, or any of the apparatus or furniture used in churning. "They take any one for a witch," we read in Camden, "that comes to fetch fire on May Day, and therefore refuse to give any, unless the party asking it be sick; and then it is with an imprecation, believing that all their butter will be stolen the following summer by this woman. On May Day, likewise, if they can find a hare among their herd, they endeavour to kill her, out of a notion that it is some old witch that has a design upon their butter."* This legend about the hare is still universally believed throughout Ireland, and must be based on some ancient general superstition. The tale goes that witches have then the power of transforming themselves into

* See also Laurence Echart's "Exact Description of Ireland." London, 1691.

hares, with the intention of more secretly and securely milking or sucking the cows; which, if they can effect, they become possessed of the power of having in their own churn, during the next twelve months, the butter of all the cows so circumstanced. You will still be told, with various readings, in almost every county in Ireland, with all the accurate recital of the names of persons and localities, how such and such an hare was once hunted, and so closely pressed by the dogs, that she was wounded in the thigh, but eventually escaped by leaping into the window of a small cabin " hard by the bog;" and how, that upon the hunters coming up and entering the hovel, lo! no hare was to be seen, but an old hag smoking her *dudeen* sat by the fire, or was rolled up in the bed-clothes, who, when examined, exhibited a recent wound, still bleeding, in identically the same part on which it had been inflicted on the hare. This legend is detailed circumstantially in Anthony Bruodine's old work, " Œcodomia Minoriticæ Scholæ Salamonis," Pragæ, 8vo, 1663. Has not the adage, " I'll make a hare of you," arisen from the belief of hares being occasionally bewitched? The *Graunogue*, or hedgehog, is worried by idle, mischievous boys, chiefly on account of the belief that it milks the cows.

Every one who can, wishes to churn before sunrise upon May morning, and those who possess the means commence their lacteal operations at an early hour; but as churning is a ceremony always attended with a certain degree of risk, whether owing to the evil influences of fairyism, or witchcraft, or, as some of our modern philosophers would have us to believe, arising from certain defects in the manipulation of this chemical process, or some deleterious qualities in the fodder or pasture of the cow, it here matters little. The fact is believed, and the precautions are taken accordingly. The cabin door is always closed, and should any person enter inadvertently, whether a stranger, or one of the family, they are at once invited to " take the dash," if only for a few minutes. To refuse would be considered, in one of the upper ranks, not only unpolite, but unlucky, and in one of the poor people, the height of witchcraft. Curious and many are the means taken by the peasants' and farmers' wives to ensure success, and to gather a plentiful *mischaun* of butter, when the milk cracks and the boiling water is added; such as putting a coal of fire and some salt under the churn, inserting a piece of charmed writing between the hoops, nailing an old ass's shoe to the bottom of the churn-dash, &c. —superstitious rites which appertain more particularly to milk and butter cures and charms, to be detailed hereafter. But the great means of averting the threatened danger resides in the employment of the mountain-ash, or rowan-tree (the *crankeeran*), for which purpose a branch or sapling of that sacred tree is procured at May Eve, and bound round the churn before the churning is commenced; and every vessel containing milk or butter, or in any way connected with the dairy, is also encircled with carefully peeled gads or switches of the same material. This rite, which is not confined to the Roman Catholics, or the lower orders, is still practised, even by the educated. Among the English settlers, who still retain the old Saxon legend of Robin Goodfellow, it is feared that he may

> ——"fright the maidens of the villagery;
> Skim milk; and sometimes labour in the quern,
> And bootless make the breathless housewife churn."

Some of the people, if asked for a reason for not permitting fire to leave the house on May Day, tell you that it is to prevent the fairies taking possession; and assign as a reason for not giving away milk, that if it was used to boil herbs, or for any charm-working purpose, particularly against the *gentry*, the cow would assuredly be taken as a substitute for the person relieved by the charm.

Do not all these observances with respect to cows, and all these precautions relating to butter and milk, go some way to establish the fact of the primitive Irish being a pastoral and cattle-feeding people?

If a person has been unwell, particularly of any chronic disease, for any length of time, "the man of the house," upon May Eve, breaks the spindle of a woollen wheel over the head of the invalid, and death or recovery is confidently anticipated therefrom within three days.

In Cork there is a custom amongst the children, especially the girls, both on May Eve and May Day, of *running a muck* with bunches of nettles, stinging every one they meet, Fortunately this is a very local amusement.

The May dew, as everyone knows, possesses peculiar virtues. If an old woman be seen gathering it in a sheet, or with a sieve, or with her hands, upon a May morning, nothing will persuade the people that she is not performing a charm by which she can steal the butter of all the cows that graze upon that pasture from which she selects it. There is only one other more efficacious mode of butter-stealing (always excepting the dead man's hand, which we shall describe another time), and that is to follow the milch-cow, as she walks either field, or road, or *boreen*, and pick up the tracks made in the soft earth by the four feet of the animal, or gather the bits of *clauber* that stick between the clefts of the feet. Should a set of these be thus acquired, the farmer may expect but a poor return of butter for the next twelve months: but if procured by the owner of the beast, she is henceforth invulnerable.

The girls rise early on the first of May, and kneeling down over the glittering gossamer,

 " Brush the light dew-drops from the spangled lawn."
and bathe their necks and faces therewith to keep off the freckles and beautify their skin, like Mr. Pepys's his wife, who went to Woolwich, in olden time, for " a little ayre, and to gather May dew." It is not alone for its cosmetic power, however, that the Irish girls employ it, as Sam. Lover has touchingly described in his " Song of the May-dew," but as a bond of peculiar power among lovers.

Cutting the May bush, upon May Eve, is one of the longest established ceremonies connected with this festival. A full-grown thorn was, in former times, generally selected; often months before the day, and no matter where it might grow, it was considered the property of the May, and to be procured at all risks, even of limb or life. Much as the people venerated, at all other times and seasons, their indigenous thorns, especially when growing on some of the ancient raths, they paid no respect to the sanctity of their character or position if marked for the May bush. In fact, in some places, the ancient thorn of what is called a fairy rath was considered more applicable than any other.   Upon May Eve a crowd of persons, often numbering several hundreds, resorted to the spot previously arranged, with saws, hatchets, ropes, cars, horses, and all the necessary tackle for cutting and carrying home the May bush, and were generally escorted by fifers and fiddlers.   Serious rencontres very often ensued upon these occasions, particularly in the neighbourhood of Dublin, where the authorities had frequently to interfere to prevent some lawn or demesne being despoiled of its wide-spreading thorn.   The trophy was, however, generally carried off in triumph, amidst the shouts and rejoicings of the people, and erected in its allotted station, and upon its branches were fixed a number of small candles, which at night-fall were lighted, and afforded a brilliant illumination for the dancers, who tripped it round this emblem of the vernal light, as is still practised in Germany on Christmas Eve.   In some parts, particularly in Monaghan, the May bush used to be erected several days before the festival, and was illuminated every night; and in addition, pyramids of "penny dips," fixed in lumps of yellow clay, used to be erected in the neighbourhood of the bush, which always stood upon some green or common, or at the cross-roads, or in the market-place of the town or village.   Early upon May morning the bush was decorated with flowers, ribbons, and pieces of silk of the most gaudy colours; and at the conclusion of the festivities the bush was consigned to the flames of the expiring bonfire.   In former days the Liberty bush was cut in Cullen's Wood.   Efforts were often made, particularly in the city of Dublin, to steal away the May bush, to avert which a guard of stout fellows was set to keep watch and ward nightly, from the time of its erection until after the festival.   The abduction of the Smithfield May bush gave rise to the old slang song to which we have already alluded at page 47, when Bill Durham, with the fishwomen of Pill Lane, sallied forth to recover the palladium of Ormondtown,—

> "From de lane came each lass in her holiday gown,
>   Riggidi ri dum dee;
> Do de haddocks was up, and de lot was knocked down,
> Dey doused all dere sieves till dey riz de half crown,
>   Ri riggidi ri dum dee."

Besides the grand May bush of the locality, each house, especially in the rural districts, had its little bush, generally a branch of thorn, decorated with flowers, and most usually placed on the dunghill, so high that any passing witch could not easily leap over it. "April showers bring May flowers" is an old saying; and their welcome has grown into the sweet proverb of "you're as welcome as the flowers in May," so charmingly harmonized by our own dear Slingsby.

The custom which has remained longest and most perfect amongst us is the floral decoration of the doors and windows, chiefly with May flowers, then found in full blow in deep meadows and moist places. This gay plant, the marsh-marigold (Catha palustris), called in Irish the shrub of Beltine, *Bearnan Bealtaine*, or the *Lus-ubrich Bealtaine*, always forms the chief ornament of the garlands and other floral decorations, and is generally strewn plentifully before the doors and on the threshold; but when such can be procured, wild flowers, white or yellow (butter or milk colour), and those that grow in meadows and pastures, are ever preferred to garden flowers, to place in the cottage windows, scatter round the doors, or adorn the May bush and May pole.

The May pole never appears to have been in general use in Ireland, and is evidently of English introduction. In Connaught it is unknown; and even those places where it obtained most repute in other parts of the country were generally English settlements, as in Westmeath, where it was constantly to be found as described by Sir H. Peirs, in "Vallancy's Collectanea."

The only authorized pole now standing which we know of is at Hollywood, near Belfast, where it is used to bear the orange-and-blue flags and streamers on the twelfth of July, equally with the flower-decked hoops and green garlands of the first of May. When we last saw it, it was decorated with miniature ships, emblematic of the calling of the villagers. There formerly existed one at Mountmellick, which was applied to a similar purpose; but that which stood upon the mall at Downpatrick, some thirty years ago, was one of the most celebrated in Ireland. Among the rites and ceremonies which attached to this latter was one somewhat similar to the privilege assumed, if not granted, under the Christmas mistletoe in England. Whenever a lady appeared in the vicinity of the May pole, or went to visit the revels upon Downpatrick mall on May Day, she was liable to be asked by any of the tradesmen present to take a turn round the pole, and, at the end of the dance, if her partner was so inclined, they concluded with a kiss. The omission of the latter part of the ceremony was often purchased with a bribe. A milk offering used, in former times, to be made at the foot of the May pole.*

The two Dublin May poles were erected outside the city. One of these stood in the centre of Harold's-cross Green, and existed within the memory of some of the present generation. After its decay, an old withered poplar supplied its place for many years; and so recently as the year 1836, the publicans of the village erected a May pole, decorated it, and gave a number of prizes, in order to collect an assemblage of the people, by restoring the ancient festivities. The chief May pole of Dublin, however, was erected at the pretty suburban village of Finglas, to the north of the city, near the Glasnevin Botanic Gardens, a spot which combines the most delicious sylvan scenery with the charm of the associations connected with the names of Swift, Addison, Tickel, Delany, and in our own day of our distinguished fellow-citizen Doctor Walsh. Here it stood until within the last few years;—a very tall, smooth pole, like the mast of a vessel, and upon every Easter Monday it was painted white and encircled with a red and blue spiral stripe like a barber's pole. In latter years, at least, it was not decorated with floral hoops and garlands like the usual English May pole, but was well soaped from top to bottom in order to render it the more difficult to climb; and to its top were attached, in succession, the different prizes, consisting generally of a pair of leather breeches, a hat, or an old pinchbeck watch. Whoever climed the pole, and touched the prize, became its possessor. "All Dublin" turned out to Finglas upon May Day to witness the sports and revels of the

---

* "Strutt's Sports and Pastimes" may be consulted with advantage by those who would wish to know more of the May Day customs in England.

people, and the streets of the little village, and the adjoining roads were thronged with carriages, hackney-cars, jingles, and noddies, filled with the better class of citizens. There were also a gaudily-dressed king and queen of the May, chosen from among the villagers, but they were the least attractive portion of the assembly. The revels consisted of climbing the pole; running after a pig with a shaved and well-soaped tail, which was let loose in the middle of the throng; grinning through horse-collars for tobacco; leaping and running in sacks; foot races for men and women; dancing reels, jigs, and hornpipes; ass races, in which each person rode or drove his neighbour's beast, the last being declared the winner; blindfolded men trying to catch a bell-ringer; and also wrestling, hopping, and leaping. An adjoining field was selected for the celebration of the majority of these sports. Stewards were appointed to keep the course, and see fair play, and twenty or thirty pounds' worth of prizes, consisting of shawls, hats, frieze-coats, hand-kerchiefs, and women's gowns and bonnets, were often dis-tributed among the winners. Tents were erected, and bands of music paraded through the assembly; and even shows and booths were to be seen scattered throughout the village. In the evening the crowds collected round the May pole, where the boys and girls danced in a ring until a late hour, before the king and queen, who, attended by a man dressed as a Highlander, sat on a raised platform. Some thirty years ago, the Finglas sports were rendered particularly attractive by the exertions of three celebrated characters—Watty Cox, the noto-rious seditious libeller; Bryan Maguire, the celebrated duel-list; and Michael Farrell, the well-known police-officer, who all lived in the neighbourhood. The May sports, however, had been gradually declining till about the year 1826, when a number of the traders and citizens of Dublin, chiefly those who had country houses in the vicinity of the village, formed themselves into a social society, at first called the "Tolka Club;" but afterwards they assumed to themselves the title of the "Corporation of Finglas," and elected a lord mayor, recorder, member of Parliament, sheriff, aldermen, and other officers, as well as a chaplain, with the title of Bishop of Fingal.* These jolly companions dined at one another's houses weekly during the summer months, and generally "made a night of it." The chief object of the institution, however, was to keep alive the May Day sports, and the *" humours "* of Finglas. More than one application was made to the government to interdict the Finglas amusements, by some of the gentry residing in the neighbourhood; and the subject was even considered grave enough to be referred to the Privy Council; but what official interference was unable to put down—first, the cholera panic, in 1833, and then teetotalism, completely abolished. The "Tolka Club" was broken up, Finglas became deserted, cold water damped the ardour of· the revellers, the king and queen of the May were threatened with the watchhouse; the festivities ceased when the prizes were omitted, and the May pole was neglected, when it, like Brian O'Lynn, "had no breeches to wear," and the old song, of which we recollect but the following verse, is now scarcely remembered :—

> "Ye lads and lasses all, to-day,
> To Finglas let us haste away;
> With hearts so light and dresses gay,
> To dance around the May pole."

The May boys and morris-dancers went their rounds, particularly in Connaught and Munster, even so late as within the last twenty years. They consisted of a dozen or two of the " cleanest and most likely " boys in the vicinity, who took off their coats, and decorated themselves with garlands, ribbons, and silk handkerchiefs of the brightest colours, generally furnished them by their sweethearts, who vied with each other in dressing their lovers to the greatest advantage. One of the most effeminate of the number was dressed in female attire as queen of the May (in the country parts we never heard of a girl having acted the part); a king or captain was appointed, as also a spokesman, who repeated the rhymes; a treasurer carried the money-box, and a fool or devil, (like that

* One of the last remaining members of the "Tolka Club" is Mr. Ross Cox, the South American traveller, to whom we are indebted for a most interesting account of this Society. The bishop was a worthy and facetious Roman Catholic clergyman, still living.

of the wren-boys and mummers at Christmas), a sort of " Lord of Misrule," cleared the way, frightened the children, bespattered the crowd, uttered the broad rustic jokes current among the people at that time, and capered for the general amusement. This person wore a sort of loose garment covered with many-coloured shreds and patches of cloth and rags tacked to it; a large, brimless hat, with the front of it formed into a hideous mask, came down over his head; a row of projecting pieces of stick made to resemble teeth surrounded the mouth; a piece of goat-skin formed the beard, and the eye-holes were surrounded by circles of red cloth. To the back of it was fastened a dried hare's skin. In his hand he carried a long wattle, to which an inflated bladder was attached, and a very formidable weapon it was, particularly against the women and children.

In the south, we understand, the May boys used to sport a female fool—a sort of Audrey for their Touchstone. Thus attired, and accompanied by fiddlers, fifers, and tambourine players, and escorted by a great concourse of idlers, the May boys used to perambulate the country for a week together at May time, visiting the different gentlemen's seats, where they danced, repeated their rhymes, and were generally entertained with true Irish hospitality. They always got a bottle of whiskey and some money, with which they made merry at their resting-place in the evening. Some parties carried a May bush before them, and sometimes they managed to seat the piper on the bush, when they commenced their rhymes. In the county of Clare, about fifty years ago, the May boys used to mount their captain or king of the May on horseback, who carried in his hand a long pole decked with ribbons and flowers, and bearing a garland at the top.

The May Day rhymes of the Irish peasantry are almost forgotten, and, in a few years hence, it is more than probable that a single verse of them will not live in the recollection of the people. They were often repeated in Irish; but the following scraps of a long, rude doggerel, which we possess, was the most general English version employed in Connaught, particularly in the counties of Roscommon and Galway:—

> "This morning as the sun did rise,
> We dressed the pole you to surprise;
> With our fiddle and our pipes so gay,
> To bring you good cheer on the first of May."

Several of the verses are but a paraphrase of the mummers and wren-boy rhymes. After describing "the treat" they expected, and hinting that—

> "If it is but of the small,
> It wont agree with the boys at all."

They added—

> "'Tis then we'll dance and drink away,
> And our pole and May bush thus display,
> Until his fine lady to us will say,
> Boys, 'tis time for you to go away;
>
> "Then we'll take off our hats and give three cheers,
> Praying she may live these fifty years,
> And off we'll go without delay,
> Playing the tune called 'The First of May.'"

The sweet old air of "The Summer is Coming," to which Moore has written the song of "Rich and rare were the gems she wore," is what was generally repeated, but we can only procure a single verse of it :—

> Saṁnaḋ, ṙaṁnaḋ, bainne na ngaṁna
> Tugaṁhan fein an ṙaṁnaḋ linn,
> An ṙaṁnaḋ buiḋe 'ran noiṁn gléigeal
> Iṙ ċugamain féin an ṙaṁnaḋ linn.

> Summer! Summer! the milk of the heifers,
> Ourselves brought the summer with us,
> The yellow summer and the white daisy,
> And ourselves brought the summer with us.

We remember a half-witted, purblind creature, known by the soubriquet of *Saura Llynn*, walking through the town of Castlerea upon May morning, playing on an old, rude bagpipe, with May flowers round his hat, and chanting this song, of which we have given above a verse in the original, the burden of which was:—

> "Saura! Saura! bonne na Gauna,
> Hugamur fain au Saura linn."

The summer was coming;—as soon as this half fool appeared, it was the general signal for all the idle boys and all the May bushers to flock round him like swallows after a hawk, so that by the time he had reached the centre of the village, he presented in his train a motley crowd. When last we heard of this poor fellow, who generally came to us from the extreme west, the only portion of his pipes which remained was the chanter, with his mouth applied to which, he used to blow a terrific squeal, then flourish it above his head, leap forwards in maniacal excitement and shout a few disjointed verses of the well-known song.

We find but slight traces of pantomime or theatrical representation among our May sports. In the south, the Mayers of former times had the hobby-horse as part of the procession; but that part of the ceremony was evidently an English importation, which has long since been lost. From Monaghan we have a graphic account of a somewhat similar proceeding; there the girls dressed up a churn-dash as a "May babby," like the *Breedeogue* at Candlemas—and the men, a pitchfork, with a mask, horse's tail, a turnip head, and ragged old clothes, as a "May boy;" but these customs have, we believe, long since become quite obsolete, as well as the following, described by Vallancy, in his "Inquiry into the First Inhabitants of Ireland:"—"In some parts, as the counties of Waterford and Kilkenny, the brides married since the last May Day are compelled to furnish the young people with a ball covered with gold lace, and another with silver lace, finely adorned with tassels; the price of these sometimes amounts to two guineas." These balls were, he says, "suspended in a hoop ornamented with flowers."

In the county of Meath, and throughout Fingal, it is customary for several boys and girls to go forth in gangs to seek for service on May morning, and particularly on the Sunday following, called there *Sonnoughing Sunday*, each one carrying some emblem of their peculiar calling; the girls always holding in their hands peeled switches or white wands; the men having something indicative of their employment—a carter a whip, a ploughboy a goad, a thresher a flail, or *boulteen*, and a herd a wattle, with a knob or crook on the end of it; or a hazel or round-tree rod, its extremity burned in the May bonfire, as a lucky staff wherewith to drive the cattle.

Certain legends relating to May Day attach to particular localities, as that of O'Donoghoe at Killarney, thus described by Crofton Croker: "On the first of May, in the morning, when the sun is approaching the summer solstice, the Irish hero, O'Donoghue, under whose dominion the golden age formerly reigned upon earth, ascends, with his shining elves, from the depths of the Lake of Killarney, and with the utmost gaiety and magnificence, seated on a milk-white steed, leads the festive train along the water. His appearance announces a blessing to the land, and happy is the man who beholds him."* "The Motty's Stone"† comes down from the Connery mountain every May morning to bathe in the Meeting of the Waters. Our good friend, Mr. R. Dowden, R. of Cork, informs us that he even saw some of the peasant children in Kerry enact the marriage of Cupid and Psyche as a part of the May Day pastime.

In addition to the foregoing may be added the following memoranda of the ancient rites and customs peculiar to May Day.

Herbs gathered on May Day are boiled with some hair from the cow's tail, and carefully preserved in a covered vessel. A small portion of this charm is put into the churn before churning, and is also smeared upon the inside of the pails before the milk is "set."

Certain herbs known only to the initiated, but including yarrow, speedwell, and a plant famous for all cattle-charms,

---

* "Fairy Legends and Traditions of the South of Ireland," part iii., p. 92.

† The Motty's Stone.—"It is said that this huge mass (which one is perplexed to know how it came to occupy its place except during the Deluge) descends every May morning to perform an ablution at the 'Meeting of the Waters,' and then pays its respects to a smaller stone, beneath a tree beside the stream. There is a peculiar virtue, or healing power, in the river at that time; for any persons who are so fortunate as to observe the descent of the stately gentleman, and subsequently plunge with him into the waters, will infallibly be cured of whatever disease afflicts them."—*Alric De Lisle; a Poem, with Notes.* By Rev. J. G. Angley. Dublin: 1842. Page 17.

which, translated into English, means "the herb of the seven cures," are boiled together, and the water given to cows with calf as a preservation against ill luck and the fairies.

Rods of mountain-ash are placed, at May Eve, in the four corners of the corn-fields, which are also sprinkled with Easter holy water. Balls of tough yellow clay, inclosing three grains of corn, used to be placed by malicious persons in the corners of their neighbours' fields, in order to blight their crops.

A stock of brooms must be laid in before May Day, as it would be unlucky to make any at May time. In case of necessity, a sheaf of straw is used instead of a broom.

In the counties of Kilkenny and Waterford, it was customary for the neighbours to go from house to house, light their pipes at the morning's fire, smoke a blast, and pass out, extinguishing them as they crossed the threshold.*

We learn that, about seventy years ago, it was customary for the people in the same locality to assemble from different baronies and parishes, in order to try their strength and agility in kicking towards their respective houses a sort of monster foot-ball, prepared with thread or wool, and several feet in circumference. To whichever side it was carried the luck of the other was believed to be transferred.

In seeking for the snail or slug alluded to at page 53, its colour is taken into account, the white being considered the most fortunate; but the hue of the little animal is said to indicate the lover's complexion.

The long dance, referred to at page 52, was in times past performed with great spirit in the county Kilkenny, at the celebrated moat of Tibberoughny, near Piltown. The assemblage—consisting of the bearers of the May bush, the dancers, musicians, and spectators—entered the moat at the south-western gap, circumambulated the outer entrenchment several times, ascended the lofty mound by the north-east path, placed the emblem of summer on the summit, and commenced the revels. The May bush, or May pole, was here adorned with those golden balls provided by the beauties married in the

* For these, and many other ancient rites and legends, we are indebted to an intelligent friend.

neighbourhood at the preceding Shrovetide, as related by Sir John Peirs, and referred to at page 67 of this work. A renowned fairy man, with a large key in his hand, led the van, and having apportioned his prescribed rounds, entered the moat, and then, taking off his hat, called in a loud sonorous voice three times, "Brien O'Shea—he—hi—ho!" Not receiving an answer, he tried another gap or door of the enchanted fort; but his second and third efforts having likewise proved unsuccessful, he, falling back upon the subterfuge of more modern conjurers and Mesmerists, said it was the wrong key he had, or that there was some mistake about the day—it was not the "raal right ould May Day." The great summer bonfire was afterwards lighted in the centre of this fort or rath.

The *Glas Gaivlen*, the sacred or fairy milk-white cow with the green spots, so famed in Irish story, and from which so many localities derive their names and legends, was generally seen on May Day, and fortunate was the farmer among whose flocks she then appeared. We intend to take up the subject of this celebrated animal at another time, and would therefore be glad to receive local information thereon.

Some of the first milking is always poured on the ground as an offering to the *good people* on May Day. It is also considered very dangerous to sleep in the open air on May Day, or any time during the month of May. Several of the diseases to which the Irish peasantry are liable are attributed to " sleeping out."

For further particulars respecting the celebration of May, Brady's " Clavis Calendaria " may be consulted.

Should any of our readers observe other rites or customs, or be acquainted with any circumstances or superstitions in addition to those which we have thrown together in the foregoing details, we entreat their corrections and amendments.

CHAPTER III.

"In Ireland a Fetch is the supernatural fac-simile of some individual which
comes to insure to its original a happy longevity or immediate dissolution; if
seen in the morning, the one event is predicted; if in the evening, the other."—
BANIM.

"To Hell or Connaught!" was a malediction well known
and often expressed in the North and East fifty years ago; the
choice of localities being generally left to the person entrusted
with the mission. We have not ventured to explore the former,
for although the way thither is clearly defined by the minis-
ters of all religious sects in this country, the return is not so
easy. Connaught, however, as the other alternative, we have
tried, having been, as the Yankees say, "raised in that pro-
vince," and are now to the fore to offer some reason for its
supposed contiguity to a more tropical region.

What the country west of the Shannon has been hereto-
fore, may be conjectured by observing, even cursorily, what it
is at the present moment; and the estimate, of a portion of it
at least, has been tolerably well defined in the late bidding for
the Connemara estates,* when, despite the puff preliminary in
the friendly invitation of a Viceroy, the puff collusive in the
speech of a London Lord Mayor, and the puff direct in the
eloquent "setting up" of the first auctioneer of the day, before
an auditory almost choking with a plethora of wealth—little
more than half their intrinsic value was offered. The *Quar-
terly* knew better than any of them, and was just out in time
to save the London millionaire from risking his fifty or sixty
thousand pounds in the dillisk, sloak, and carrigeen moss on

* This chapter was written in the autumn of 1849, shortly after the events
alluded to in the text had occurred.

the rocks and cliffs, from Roundstone to Slimehead, or in growing flax upon the serpentine and granite of the twelve pins of Bennabola. But what's the use in going over the same story, and ringing the famine and fever, and poor-law desolation in your ears, good Christians, again;—Sure I told you how it was with all Ireland when I discoursed you before on the same subject as the present; and if you want to know how Connaught is now, I can tell you that it is ten times worse—only that the people (and more is the wonder) are ·honester, more peaceable, and although given a trifle to lying, bear starvation with less grumbling than in any other part of the world where human beings are subjected to like misery, and have so long suffered from the same demoralizing influences.

No one will buy in Connaught now ;—it is said they cannot. Why ? Certainly English capitalists, some of them of great name, who have lately visited this country, have assured us that it was not the ill-conditioned state of the peasantry—nor the desolate appearance of the country—nor the debts due by the landlords, no—nor the want of title, or the defect of drainage—nor of means of access—nor even the low price of corn—nor the danger to life or property :—all these could be calculated upon; their probable losses and profits summed up; and when a "view" was made of the whole, it would be found to be just worth, like any other property, so many years' purchase, and would bring its proper price in the market; but it was the taxation which they dreaded, the poor-law taxation of which they could form no estimate, even for the next couple of years,—a taxation which, it is feared, may soon increase to such an extent as to exceed the fee-simple of the land. Well, this is all very true; but this taxation is to feed the people,—will it not increase as the population increases ? Yes, but the population *will not, cannot increase under the present circumstances.* Already it has been thinned to an extent almost unparalleled under any condition of the country, as will be proved when the next census is taken.* We now speak of the

---

* The results of the late census have fully verified this opinion. The loss in Connemara has been 16,493 : in the barony of Ballynahinch, 9119 ; and 7374 in that of Moycullen.

West, with which we have been long familiar, and we venture to assert that, within two years from the present, the numbers which will have taken advantage of poor-law relief, and who must consequently be a burden upon the land, will have reached, if not passed, the maximum; and as the numbers requiring relief, either within doors or without, shall be thinned and decreased, so ought the taxation to lessen also.

We lately made a tour of the West, after an absence of twelve years. What have we seen—what was the impression made upon us in passing through districts with which we have been long familiar? This—that until the late potato failure and consequent famine, there must have been immense agricultural improvement going forward even in Connaught; for, although we passed over miles of country without meeting the face of a human being, and seldom that of a four-footed beast, and though we came, in some places, hot upon the smoking ruins of a recently unroofed village, with the late miserable inmates huddled together and burrowing for shelter among the crushed rafters of their cabins; and although there were large tracts of land untilled and untenanted—still, with the traces of cultivation, far beyond what we remember in former times, passing under our eyes; with improved drainage—in many places rendering the former swamp a meadow; with the dark patches of green crops creeping up the sides of the valleys; with the turnip, the cabbage, and the parsnip surrounding the cottage, where alone the potato had a footing previously; and, with large tracts of bog reclaimed wherever there was an improving, and, consequently, a wise and humane as well as thriving landlord*—we could not but feel that the appearance of the country, generally, had improved since 1837. But, to the subject of the depopulation,—

Thousands of the peasantry have died annually since 1846,

* No better proof of this could be adduced than the present condition of the tongue of land—part of the Barnah property, in Connemara, running in from Ballinakille bay to the shores of Kylemore Lake, and now in the possession of Mr. Graham; on one side of it is the Ballynahinch estate, and on the other the Renville—both worse off than they were ten years ago—while this tract, which we remember red bog and heathy moor, is now growing corn and green crops, and has several snug homesteads upon it.

over and above the usual standard of mortality, which, in Ireland, according to the only data yet accessible, did not, upon an average, exceed two per cent. at the utmost. Thousands upon thousands of the best and most productive of the population have emigrated; and among those who remain, and who have eked out a most miserable existence without the walls of the poor-house, the births, as a natural consequence of the unhappy condition in which the country has been, have been lessened to an extent scarcely credible; and marriages—as the priests know to their cost—have fallen off beyond the remembrance of any former time. The few still standing out among the peasantry, clinging with delusive hope to the potato, and still holding on, in chronic starvation, to two acres and a-half of ill-tilled land, with that longing for liberty—but, alas! not for independence—which made the Irish peasant rather die than quit his native hearth; those supported upon public works, where such exist, or who have been receiving from the, as yet, unpauperized landlord five-pence a-day, " without mate or drink," for the few months of spring or harvest, will all have been driven into the poor-house before the beginning of 1853; while those who can muster the price of their passage to New York, either by honest accumulation or by robbing their landlords of the crops, will likewise have emigrated.

Let us go into the poor-houses, and walk through the day-wards, and yards, and workshops. We see there two classes : the worn-down peasantry, with broken constitutions, spectres of men and women, listlessly stalking about—moody, unoccupied, brooding over miseries past, without hope for the future; fit recipients, mentally and corporeally, for all the contagious influences necessarily attendant upon the accumulation of such a crowd of human beings : we feel assured, upon looking at them, that the great majority will never number another year. For the other section of this class—the boys and girls, and young men and women—many of them intelligent and with good constitutions, now growing up in the work-houses, and acclimatised to them : we feel that something must be done by legislative enactment, either to provide for them in the colonies, or to transplant them again throughout the unpopulated districts, or to hire them out as farm-servants—their legitimate and proper calling—before two years elapse; or the land must be taken by the poor-law authorities on which to employ them. And the day will come, and it is not far distant, when, unless Ireland be converted into one great grass-farm, the farmer must go to the workhouse to seek labourers for his harvest.

But there is another portion of the poor-house which we have yet to visit—the hospital. Here, whether it be a temporary shed, or the ordinary ward accommodation, as we pass down the long room, between the rows of beds, and cast our eyes on the thirty or forty human beings arranged on each side of us, a glance practised to disease assures us, that ere to-morrow's sun has set, many of the miserable beings through whom we have passed will have ceased to feel the burning fever or the wasting dysentery: their corpses will lie in the dead-house. The doctor who accompanies us will confirm our remarks. The wards are almost always full; some recent cases from without, others occurring among the broken-down paupers in the house, rapidly filling up the vacancies which every four-and-twenty hours produce. In truth, the mortality which has taken place during the last three or four years, and which is still going forward, to a certain extent, in the poor-houses of Ireland, is beyond belief. We have no desire that it should now be made known. No doubt it will be published at the proper time, and in the proper place. It is not for the sake of exciting angry feelings against these institutions that we write: we believe that, under the circumstances, the mortality has not been greater there than might have been expected; but we have made these statements because we have witnessed what we relate, and because the sum of our inquiries and observations assures us, that the number of persons requiring poor-law relief will begin to decrease, after a very few years, to an extent of which no idea can, at present, be formed. And then taxation will not fall as heavily, nor with that uncertainty which the Irishman who sells, or the Englishman who would buy land, now imagines.

Why the rulers of the West, if they have not earned for it

the adage, " To Hell or Connaught," have, at least, assisted to keep up, and, in part, to deserve, the malediction, may be gleaned from the sequel to the following tale, which, while it serves to illustrate a peculiar Irish superstition, details an historical fact, known at this very hour to hundreds where the circumstances occurred, and the proofs of which—in all save the supernatural appearances, probably the result of an excited imagination—are undeniable, and could be produced.

The reader acquainted with Irish local history may form some idea of the state of Connaught at the period to which this tale refers, and the barbarous condition of the country at the time, when we tell him, that it was many years after some of the gentry—not the " good people," but the landed proprietors, the so-called gentlemen—of Mayo, having overpowered the guards, broke into the jail of Castlebar, and attempted to assassinate one of the prisoners, whom they left for dead.* And it occurred a few years before one of the members for the county of Galway, a magistrate and a deputy-lieutenant, was tried, sentenced, and imprisoned several months, for heading a riotous armed mob; marching off with them many miles through a neighbouring town, and taking illegal and forcible possession of an acre of bog, whereby several persons were severely injured, and the peace of the realm disturbed † And it was about this time, or shortly after it, that a gentleman, then residing not far from the town of Roscommon, abducted a drove of pigs from a neighbouring magistrate with whom he happened to be dining : for which crime he was transported for life—a life he, after a long space of time, forfeited to the

* See the trial of the celebrated George Robert Fitzgerald, in 1786; and "of Timothy Brecknock, James Fulton, and others, for the procurement of, and for the murder of Patrick Randal M'Donnell and Charles Hickson ; and also the trial of John Gallagher and others, for an assault on George Robert Fitzgerald, in the Gaol of Castlebar." Dublin : printed by P. Byrne. See also " The Life of George Robert Fitzgerald." in the Dublin University Magazine, for July, August, and September, 1840, and lately republished as one of this series of popular works.

† The Battle of the Bog occurred in 1837, at Oughterard, between some of the tribe of the " Ferocious O'Flaherties," of H-Iar Connaught, and the retainers of Ballynahinch ; Thomas Martin, Esq., M.P. and J.P., the last male descendant of " Nimble Dick," having led the van, against a friend and relative of my own.

offended laws of a penal colony. Not many years ago, his son —who had been a cabin-boy at the battle of Navarino—proved in the public court-house of Leitrim, that he was the rightful heir to the estates of a man who had then but recently filled the office of high sheriff of the county, but whom a jury believed to be a supposititious child, the son of a pipe-maker.* We well remember, when a boy, seeing a lady's white satin dress be-dabbled with the blood of a dying game-cock, as she stood in the pit of a cock-fight, which formed part of the amusements got up to do honour to the coming of age of a nobleman, who was afterwards murdered in England.

Of the state of Mayo, even thirty years ago, some idea may be formed from the knowledge of the fact, that no sooner had the judges of the land left the county-town after each assizes, than a certain very celebrated character, who figures in the conclusion of this tale, went to the jail and re-ruled the books, imposing severer punishments on some, and remitting those already awarded to others by the constituted authorities. Lord Chancellor Plunket once went the Connaught circuit as judge. The redoubted ruler of Mayo sat beside him on the bench. There was a general jail delivery at the conclusion of the assizes, and all the untried prisoners were put forward in the dock to be discharged, in the usual manner, by proclamation. *The Right Honourable*, for by such appellation he was known, seeing rather an obnoxious character among them, turned to the presiding judge and said :—

" Surely, my Lord, you are not going to let Tim Muldoon, that ill-looking fellow in the corner there, loose on the world."

" Pray, Mr. B——, what accusation can you bring against him ; for the crime for which he was imprisoned appears to be so slight, that the law officers of the crown have not thought it necessary to prosecute him, or put the country to the expense of a trial."

" Oh, he is the greatest vagabond in the whole country; he is a noted ribbonman and cock-fighter; he plays the fiddle at all the wakes and dances; he is, moreover, a most determi-

---

* See the trials of Keon v. Keon, in Roscommon, Leitrim, and Galway, from 1828 to 1833.

nate poacher; he would not leave a hare in the county, and he is always engaged in illicit distillation. If you let him out, no man would be safe in the kingdom."

"But, Mr. B——, I don't find any distinct charge or indictment against him, so I must discharge him with the others."

The Right Honourable having gained a few minutes delay descended to the dock, and after holding a short conference with the prisoner returned to the bench, and gravely informed the judge that he had arranged matters with Tim Muldoon, who, he said, "has consented to plead guilty without trial to any indictment that may be extemporaneously preferred against him—provided your lordship undertakes not to transport him for longer than seven years."

The judge rose up, and with all that dignity of manner and solemnity of accent which few could exhibit with greater effect, desired Tim to be put forward, and then told him he was discharged. Great was the poor culprit's amazement after the bargain he had so recently concluded with the uncompromising western ruler.

"Whe, then, your worship's raverence;—me lady, I mane;—och your lordship; but you're an illigent gintleman all out, and its much wantin' ye were to these parts; but might I make bould jist to ax yer honor wan favor afore I go."

"Yes, my man," said Plunket, "if it is anything the law or the court can do for you, you may demand it."

"Oh, thin, 'tis you are the laughey and the asey spoken gintleman entirely. I'll tell you what it is thin. Just keep the Right Honourable where he is sittin' there beside you, fare and asey for the next twinty minutes, till I get clear of the town of Castlebar; for if you did n't, be me soukins, he'd have me be the scruff of the neck, and he'd ram me into the stone jug afore you'd say Jack Robison."

And so he would, for such were his notions of "law and order" at the time to which we refer.

Tim Muldoon vaulted out of the dock, and was never heard of since; but from that hour the power and the terror of "the big man" over the people of Mayo waned, and was never again in the ascendant. Verily, we have been a peculiar people in Connaught; and, shall we not add, zealous of bad works. These little, but truthful memorabilia may, however, serve to remind some of our friends of whom, and of what times, we write.

Connaught generally, and Roscommon in particular, was the scene of one of those paroxysms of outrage, the result of secret association, that in different localities, and at divers times, have affected the Irish peasantry, sometimes for one object, sometimes for another; a war against tithes, or, more properly speaking, tithe proctors, or against landlords and agents, or on account of con-acre, or to aid in getting emancipation or repeal to tenant right—often without any cause that even the people themselves could assign. Hence arose the Hearts-of-Steel, Caravats, and Shanavests, the Croppies, Defenders, Chalkers, Houghers, White Boys, Right Boys, Peep-o'-Day Boys, Carders,* Hacklers, Trashers, Rockites, Ribbonmen, Terry-Alts, and Molly Maguires.

Some idle malcontent, labouring under the smart of a real or supposed grievance, some pot-house agitating demagogue, some mere pecuniary speculator or tatterdemallion, obliged, for crimes of his own, to be "on the run," and seek shelter in a different county, has frequently stirred up a hitherto peaceable peasantry to band themselves into a secret society, to meet in ribbon lodges, to assume certain nicknames, to organize and arm, to have secret signs and passwords, by which the initiated might be recognized at fair or market, when a grip of the hand, or a nudge of the elbow, the way in which a man carried the tail or skirts of his *big coat*, hitched up the waistband of his breeches, lifted his glass, or knocked his quart upon the public-house table when he wanted more drink; the manner in which he cocked his hat, or handled his blackthorn; or some casual or apparently unimportant word thrown out in passing the way, as " God save you," or " the time of day," or the ordinary salutation among the lower orders, were all used as means of recognition.

---

* One of the cards, or hackles, with spikes on it an inch and a half long, which used to be hammered into the back, and then dragged down along the spine, is still in the collection of antiquities of a gentleman in Mullingar.

There is a freemasonry—a craft, or mystery, in all this, which, quite independent of other objects, possesses a charm for the human mind; and this alone will gain proselytes at all times, and among all classes, descending from the magi and heathen priests of old through the illuminati of later days, down to the various secret societies, or bodies possessing secret signs, symbols, or passwords, among the educated classes at present, either recognized by the law, or connived at by the officers of justice. We repeat it, there is a charm in this state of things which has lured many a young and innocent peasant into the snare of designing men. Besides these, there are the evil disposed at all times—the revengeful of the lower classes, the timid, and the wavering, who will each, for their respective motives, join any illegal society which may start up in their vicinity. Where and when we allude to, murder, and crimes of such debasing nature, formed no part of the ribbon system. Agrarian outrage was not known. There was no famine, the people were well fed and comfortably clothed, there were no harsh evictions, such as were lately recorded daily, neither had the clearing system then come into full operation; drunkenness was not rife, but too frequently the cruel and unmeaning practice of houghing cattle marked the progress of the epidemic. Some Manchester delegate generally commenced the work, the village schoolmaster wrote out and copied the regulations, oaths were administered, the peaceable and well-disposed were compelled, under fearful penalties, to join, the people assembled on some neighbouring hill, or on a lonesome road, at dead of night, an old pensioner drilled, marched, and counter-marched the corps; and yet, though the system of military training has been so long resorted to by Irish insurgents, we cannot record an instance in which it has been of the slightest use to those so trained.

The peasantry now became cautious, reserved, and gloomy. Faction fights ceased at fairs and markets, men drank in the backs of tents, and in the upper rooms of public-houses, and conversed in low tones, and generally in Irish. Ill-spelled Rockite notices, signed " Liftinint Starlite," or " Corporlar Moonbame," were posted on public places. Abducting horses, and riding them in the "cavalry," during the entire night, upon some embassy, to a distant part of the country, and then leaving them in a pound, with a notice to the owner of their whereabouts, was continually resorted to. But the grand feature of the ribbonism of that day was of a dramatic nature. Decorations and processions chiefly characterized the Connaught disturbances about the years 1823 and 1825. The men wore white shirts outside their clothes, or displayed scarfs or shawls of some kind, and invariably had white bands on their hats, and were otherwise adorned with ribbons of as many colours as could be procured, tied upon their hats and arms, like the Spanish contrabandista—as if to form the better mark for the soldiers with whom they might come in contact—and all dressed in their best attire for these nightly promenades.

It was really a sort of melo-dramatic exhibition. Those who wore cut paper round their hats, as wren-boys, when they grew up to be young men decorated themselves with ribbons and white shirts to act the May-boys—and, as mummers, painted their faces, and went through the Christmas pantomime with old rusty swords. These were the mechanists, stage-managers, wardrobe-keepers, dressers, scene-shifters, and " property " manufacturers of the Roscommon ribbonmen. There was a frolic, and a spirit of rude enterprise and adventure in meeting, thus attired, with an old gun, or a yeoman's rusty halbert, of a November night, and marching, by moonlight, to the sound of the fiddle or bagpipes, though what end was to be obtained thereby, the great majority of them neither knew nor cared. The people had long been taught that there was no law or justice for the poor man, unless his master was a magistrate, or, what would be still better, had an " ould family grudge " with an opposing magistrate, or that the priest would interfere in his behalf. That Irishmen were ill-treated, and got no fair play, was well known; that it was right to do something for O'Connell and the Emancipation, was firmly impressed on all; and to put down the tithe-proctors, was believed to be a most meritorious act, and for " the good of the country." But what was to be ultimately obtained by these organisations, either by themselves or others, I say again, they had no very distinct idea;—the people were, generally, the dupes of others; for what purpose we have no desire now to discuss.

Unfortunately there was, and still is, but little work for the Irish cottager or small farmer from the beginning of November till the end of February; and what little might be done, partly from ignorance and partly from apathy, he does not do; so that except when he went to the fair or the market, or was compelled to go to the bog for a *clieve* of turf, or had occasion to *put a face** on a pit of potatoes, he slept most of his days, and went out with "the boys" at night.

To oppose this state of things there were the local magistrates, and in the larger towns the military; but except when brought for some special purpose, or to attack a large collection of the people, these latter were of little use in subduing insurrection. The usual class of spies and informers soon began to ply their trade, and one of the first acts of the magistrates was to prevent or disperse all merry-makings and amusements of the people. Tents and *standings*† were pulled down at an early hour, public-houses cleared, and all assemblies dispersed; hurlings and football playing, which generally took place on Sundays or holidays, were strictly interdicted, but the ire of the authorities was chiefly directed against *cakes* ‡ and dances. When information was obtained with respect to the locality of one of these, thither the magistrate, with his| *posse comitatus*, repaired, broke into the assembly, dispersed the merry-makers, spilled the whisky, danced on the fiddle, and carried off to the

---

* "To put a face" on anything means to begin, or broach; as, for instance, to commence the removal of a ridge of potatoes, or a stack of hay, or a clamp of turf.

† "Standings," the covered booths or open-air shops, in which "soft goods" are exhibited at fairs and markets. Every method of displaying merchandise, even that of a basket or a stall, was styled a standing,—from the ass-cart, propt with a barrel, and covered over with a patch-work quilt stretched on bent rods, underneath which sat, on hunkers, the owner, surrounded with her wares—skallions, tin porringers, remnants of checks, and "ready-me-daisys"—to the regularly boarded shop, covered over with canvas or sail-cloth, in which corduroys, book-muslins, and fancy prints were displayed. Many a splendid fortune has been commenced in one of these.

‡ Cakes, the peasants' balls and suppers. See page 14.

nearest blackhole, or guard-room, the owners of the house.*
Really the only available, or permitted amusements, were
wakes and funerals—on which account some of the latter were
mock. The only available force were the old barony constables
—generally superannuated pensioners from the yeomanry or
militia; always Protestants, and most of them foresters, *cleevins*,
old servants, or hangers-on of the magistrate—who dressed in
long blue surtout coats, with scarlet collars, buckskin breeches,
and rusty top-boots. Each of these old men was mounted, and
carried a heavy cavalry sword, his only weapon, for he was
seldom fit to be entrusted with any other. Two or three of
these *fogies* might be seen at fairs, patterns, and markets,
riding up and down to keep the peace, which, as soon as the
superintending magistrate had gone to dinner, they generally
broke by getting gloriously drunk. This the people usually
bore, however, with good humour, seldom injuring the con-
stable, but affording themselves much amusement by *welting*
with shillelaghs and blackthorns their crusty nags, which,
knowing perfectly what was about taking place, immediately
commenced *lashing*, as if aware that the time was come for the
farce, although during the previous portion of the day they
remained as sober as their masters.

So daring had the ribbonmen become, that although several
had already been transported from the dock, and others had
been whipped at carts'-tails, large bodies of the insurgents

* We have just received the following from a distinguished member of the Con-
naught bar :—"Bryan Kyne was a justice of the peace for three counties. He
was tried before Baron Smith, in Roscommon, at the summer assizes of 1830; and
the case against him was, that he went to the cabin of an old man, who lived by
fiddling for the country people as they danced, and who had a crowd of them
assembled, and engaged at that amusement, on a Sunday evening, which Kyne
thought he should disperse. On his entering the cabin, he seized the fiddle,
and desired the dancers to disperse, which they did at once without a murmur.
He had a gun in his hand ; and when, by their voices, as they moved away from
the cabin, he judged that they were yet within shot, he levelled his gun in the
direction they were taking towards their homes, and injured several of them.
The principal witness was a very decent-looking youth, about twenty. He took
off his shirt, and showed his back to the judge and jury, as he stood on the table
in the public court ; and although it was nearly six months after the transaction,
it exhibited a shocking appearance of scars and cicatrices. Kyne was convicted,
and transported for life."

approached the small towns in the night time, committing several petty outrages : pulling down pound gates, and letting out the cattle, beating drivers, and warning process-servers ; so that the quiet and loyal inhabitants had to form themselves into corps, which appointed watches, and had patroles guarding their houses. Just then Peel's Act came into force; the first Peelers, under the command of the redoubted Major ——, entered Connaught, and here our story commences.

The Major, who took no inconsiderable part in the fearful drama which shortly after followed, had originally belonged to a celebrated militia regiment, of one of the midland counties, that was the first to run out of Castlebar on the approach of the French, but having stopped to take breath at Hollymount, and the men having refreshed themselves with some of the claret purloined from the cellars of the neighbouring gentry, they became suddenly seized with a fit of *nationality !* and, turning their coats inside out, they erected, in the demesne of Lehinch, a pole, crowned with a cap of liberty, round which they drank, danced, and sang till morning's dawn, when many of those who were able to march, or even to stagger, retraced their steps to join Humbert. These renegades made, however, but a bad business of it afterwards at Ballinamuck, and their subsequent *liberality* provoked the parody upon the well-known air of " Croppies lie down;" so spirited a quick step, that we greatly regret it is still remembered as a party tune.

> " Oh! the Longford militia walked into Athlone,
> And the first tune they play'd was let croppies alone ;
> Croppies get up, for you're long enough down,
> We'll thrash all those orange dogs out of the town.
>   Down, down, Orange lie down."

Paddy Welsh was a roving blade—peculiar in everything— in habits, in temper, in thought, in appearance, in expression, but especially in gait—one of the class known only to those well acquainted with the peasantry of this country—thoroughly and peculiarly Irish. By trade—oh! Paddy had no trade—he was not a tradesman, if by that term is meant a sober mechanic, following his special calling from week's end to week's end—Sundays, holidays, whole Mondays, and half Saturdays excepted—in pulling wax-ends, thickening hats, or stitching frieze, turning hacks and pearns, or in building walls, plaining planks, hooping churns, or shoeing horses. No, he could, it is true, perform each and all of these feats at a pinch just as well as many, and better than some of those that had served their time to the trade; but he had no genius for such common, continuous, everyday avocations. Neither was he an agriculturist; he held land it is undeniable, and had a snug house upon it, built by his own two hands, but that was for the wife and children, and the farm was generally tilled by "the woman of the house," "the little boy," and an occasional hired servant, with a lift now and then from a neighbour or two at the sowing and digging of the potatoes. Neither was he a trader or a dealer, at least as a legitimate calling. Sometimes when pigs were "looking up," he jobbed upon a few slips from market to market, and may be turned a pound into a thirty-shilling note thereby; but pig-jobber he was not.

If Paudeen Brannagh (Anglice, Patrick Welsh) had any special calling more than another, he was a hackler, as was his father before him, from whom he inherited (all the poor man had to leave) the best-tempered pair of hackles in the country. With these Paddy, in his younger days, when flax was much grown in Connaught, and before he became an adept at another line of life, might be seen traversing the country, his little hackle-boxes, resembling creepy stools, slung across his shoulders, one hanging behind and another before, and seeking occupation wherever there was "flax a-breaking." *

* After the flax had been steeped in the bog-hole, and bleached on the *anough*, it was taken home, kiln-dried, and in process of time broken, preparatory to being hackled, scutched, and spun into yarn; all which processes were the result of household manufactory. The flax was generally broken by men; a large stool, such as that used for a table in the peasant's cabin, was everted and laid flat on the floor. The operator sat down behind it, with a leg across each end; placed the sheaf of dried flax along the stool, holding it into the fork of the legs, and with a long stout beetle broke up the outer husk or cuticle of the fibre, preparatory to its removal, by being drawn through the hackle pins. As several persons were generally engaged in the operation at a time, the noise produced thereby was quite deafening, and hence the common expression in Connaught, indicative of great uproar—it was like " flax a-breaking."

Though Paddy was not a tradesman, nor a labourer, nor a dealer, nor any great scholar either, he was an artist—a thing, by the way, he never heard of—uneducated brute! He knew nothing of the "holiness of art," nor the purifying effects of art, nor the religious influence of art, nor mediëval ages and illuminated missals—the likes were never heard of in Connaught in those days. There was no definition of such in the old whitey-brown-papered Tommy-and-Harry-illustrated, rough-cast-covered Universal Spelling Book, nor in "The Genteel Letter-writer and Young Gentleman's True Principles of Politeness," sewed up into the back of it. Where would he hear of it? His special trade of hackling he had by hereditary descent from his father; his readings were confined to "Raymond the Fox," "The Irish Rogues and Rapparees," "Moll Flanders," "The History of Freney the Robber," and "The Battle of Aughrim,"—the latter a play of some merit, and not only much read, and frequently committed to memory, by the more intelligent of the peasantry, but also at times enacted in barns and unoccupied houses in the small towns and villages. He was an artist, nevertheless,—a fisherman,—the best we ever met; and that is a great saying. For knowing where to find trout, when and how to get them, what to rise them with, and how to play and kill them, we never met his equal. He had other accomplishments, to be sure: he was a good shot, and could creep upon a flock of grey plover, driving an old cow or a horse before him to screen him from the wary birds, with any other man in the barony. He was n't a bad fiddler either, particularly at a *rousin'* tune—"Moll in the Wad," "Rattle the Hasp," "The Grinder," or any of the classic, but now almost forgotten, airs of Connaught. He could feed, and clip, and spur, and "hand" a cock with any man that ever stood in the pit of an Easter Monday. There was n't a *pile* nor a *stag* in the three parishes but he knew its whole seed, breed, parentage, and education. Barring Pat Magreevy, he was the greatest authority on such matters from "the Barony" * to

* The Barony of Athlone is always styled, in Roscommon, *The Barney*, and contra-distinguished from the rich plains, which are called *The Maghery*. The county Roscommon was famed for cock-fighting in former days, particularly upon Easter week; and in the locality alluded to, it is not yet quite extinct.

Sliebe Bawn, and no *main* was ever fought without his presence; but latterly he did n't like to have the subject *evened* to him, by reason of a false accusation made against him by an enemy, some years before, of having stolen, out of the county Sligo, a game chicken that had been hatched in a scald-crow's nest;—but enough of that.

Among the many popular superstitions attendant upon the breeding and rearing of game fowl, it was believed that if an egg was extracted from a hawk's or raven's, or a hooded crow's nest, and a game egg placed therein, that nothing could beat the bird so reared,—that it always partook of the carnivorous propensity and indomitable courage of its nurse and the foster family with which it had been brought up.

Like St. Patrick's aunt, Misther Welsh "undherstud dishtillin'," though he seldom undertook the office of illicit distiller; but whenever anything went wrong with the ordinary manufacturer, when the burnt beer had too great a tack, or the wash rose into the still-head, or ran through the worm, he knew what to do with it, and could keep it down with a dead chicken, or something worse; and he was famed for making the best *lurrogue*, or luteing, to keep in the liquor in an old leaky still, of any other person in the seven parishes; but, we repeat, he was not by trade a distiller.

Paddy was great at a wake, where his arrival was hailed as would be that of Strauss or Lanner in a folks-ball at the Sperl or Goldenen Piern at Vienna, for nobody knew the humours of that festival beyond Paudeen Brannagh. He could tell them how to slap,* and play forfeits, and shuffle the brogue, and rehearse "the waits;" or he could sing the "Black Stripper,"†

There was a *main* fought at Boyle last year. Carlow was also celebrated for cock-fighting. About forty years ago, the following attractive notice might be seen in a cutler's window in London—"Carlow spurs sold here."

* Among the humours of a wake, the *small play* of slapping was one of the most popular. The person who was doomed, as a forfeit, to the infliction, had to stand with the back of his hand laid upon the small of his back, while each person in the game gave it the severest blow with the palm which they were able. We shall take up the subject of the wake games when considering the ceremonials attendant upon death, and would, in the meantime, be glad to receive from our friends some information upon the subject.

† Allegories were not confined to the learned in Ireland. The "Bleeding

and "Nell Flaherty's Drake," or repeat a rhan beyond compare. The young, and those unconcerned in the mournful spectacle, welcomed him with loud applause; even those in grief would smile through their tears, and the nearest relative of the deceased would exclaim :—

"Oh, thin, musha Paddy, you *summahawn*, bad cess to you, is it here you're coming with your tricks, and we in grief and sorrow this night?"

"Hould your whist, sthore ma chree, sure it's for that I stept over, just to keep ye from thinking, and to anose the colleens.   Never mind till you see how I'll dress the garlands, and curl the paper for you coming on morning."   For this was one of Pat's accomplishments.   He could assist the women to lay out the corpse; but in case of the death of a young un-married person, he could peel, and dress with cut paper, the sally wands to be carried at the funeral, and could shape the white-paper gloves which were to hang on the hoops—the principal decoration of the garland that was to be placed in the middle of the grave.   Full of fun and frolic as he was, he was always doing a good turn, and everybody said—"There is no harm in life in him."

Paddy stood five feet nothing in his stocking-feet—no, not that either—in his barefoot; first, because he never had feet to his stockings, and secondly, because, if he put both feet to the ground, he would be nearly six inches lower than the standard we have assigned to him; for, owing to some natural defect, his left leg was by so much shorter than his right.   To com-mence with his lower extremities, which were the most remarkable feature about him, we must inform our readers that he wore neither brogues, pumps, shoes, galouches, nor boots, neither Hessians, tops, nor Wellingtons; but a pair of short-

Iphiginia," or the "History of Cyprus," or the beautiful expressive song of the "Wild Geese," which were intended and adapted for the reading population, had their types among the lower orders in such songs as the "Black Stripper," which signified a potteen still.   This song was made by a poor poet near Elphin, upon the celebrated St. Lawrence, the gauger, of Strokestown, the most noted still-hunter in Connaught for many years.   It was for a long time the most popular ballad throughout Roscommon and Leitrim, and you heard it as fre-quently wherever there was an assemblage of the people, as but a little while ago our ears were assailed with "Rory O'More."

laced buskins, made by a brogue-maker, which caused all the difference to the wearer in the matter of economy.*

He was vain (who is not?), and consequently never attempted the *knees* and long stockings, but clad his nether man in corduroys, or *borrogue*, a sort of coarse, home-made twilled linen, formed of tow-yarn. His only other garment— at least the only other one which we could discover that he wore for many years—was an old whitish, drab-coloured, double-caped greatcoat, the long skirts of which, first rolled into a sort of twisted rope, were then tucked up below the small of his back, where they formed a sort of male bustle, which, with his fiddle stuck under it, and the acquired set of an eager and habitual fisherman, gave him an extraordinary angular appearance. A sharp, shrewd countenance, prominent nose and cheek-bones—small, keen grey eyes, expressive of naturally great, as well as long-practised observation—a face which would have exhibited as many freckles as a turkey's egg, but that it was, particularly in summer time, too much tanned and sunburnt to let them be seen, exhibited at once hardihood and cunning. The peculiar chestnut hue of his face—the result of constant exposure to wind and sun—descended, like a gorget, to about the middle of his chest, over a remarkably prominent throat, in which, if Paddy inherited his peculiarity of a remark- ably projecting larynx from mother Eve, more than half of the apple must have stuck in her throat.† Whiskers he had none, but scanty beard, and scarcely a vestige of eyebrow. To make up, however, for the want of hair upon this portion of his face, he possessed a peculiar power over the part whereon it should

* The difference between a brogue and a shoe does not altogether consist in the strength of the material. Like a brogue, a shoe may be made very strong, and be unbound ; but the former is generally made of what is called *kip*, a sort of thin cow-hide, and is always unbound and unlined. The grand difference between it and a shoe consists in the sole and welt being sown together with a thong of leather instead of a wax-end. The two trades were quite distinct a few years ago.

† There is a popular impression that the peculiar prominence on the front of the throat which some persons, particularly those of red or sandy hair, exhibit, is a remnant of a deformity transmitted to us from Eden ; as it is believed that a piece of the apple stuck in Eve's throat, where it ever after remained, an eye-sore and a curse. In some localities, it is said the bit stuck, not in Eve's, but in Adam's throat.

have grown; for he could elevate it, particularly toward the outward side, half way up his forehead and temples, and again depress it so as almost completely to obscure his eye. Although his face was thus devoid of hair, he possessed a plentiful head of tow-like wool, of a yellow, sandy colour, which was generally surmounted by an old glazed hat, rather battered in the sides, and invariably encircled, during the fishing season, with casting-lines and trout flies. Oh! what a business it was for some of the young tyros to engage Paddy in conversation about the effects of the last flood, or whether there was too much rain overhead, or how long the dry weather would last, or when the green-drake would be out, or to get him to tell the story of the otter that seized the trout he was playing under the bridge of Balloughoyague, while the others, creeping carefully round, examined what hackles and foxes, or fiery-browns and hares' ears, he had last been fishing with. The genteel part of Paddy was his hand. No lady of gentle blood, or pure aristocratic descent, ever possessed a more delicate finger, or a finer touch. Signs on him, he was the boy that could mount a Limerick hook on a stout bristle, and mix the colour, strip a hackle, or divide a wing with e'er an angler in Connaught. The real wonder about Paddy was his extraordinary powers of progression. Although a *baccough*, no one could beat him "at the long run" on the road; and as to crossing a country, we could never tell how he got over the fences, or passed the drains, but he was always as soon as his companions.

Some folks accused Paddy of being a poacher; but this we stoutly deny. He would go any distance to destroy a net, or inform upon the owner of one; but wherever manual dexterity or adroitness were called in question, he had no qualms as to the means employed. Thus, if Paddy was sauntering by the river of a hot, bright, calm summer's day, when no trout in its senses would rise, and that he saw a good lump of a fish standing, or balancing itself in a still pool, or lying in the shade of a weed or rock, he at once set off after a neighbouring cow, which he soon inveigled into a ditch, or pinned in a corner, that he might pull a lock of hair from her tail, with which, fastened upon the end of a long switch, he soon formed a snare, slipped it adroitly over the gills of the unsuspecting fish, and in an instant lifted it out of its native element; or, if that was not attainable, he would walk into the stream, even to his middle, in the hope of *tickling* the trout under a stone.

Paddy's residence was on the banks of the Suck, in the gentle fords and long deep retches of which, between Ballymoe and Castlecoote, through the deep alluvial pastures of Roscommon, he plied his skilful angle between spring and summer, and in winter he shot great quantities of duck, teal, and widgeon. His house was approached by a deep narrow *boreen*, generally so wet and muddy that one had to walk on the top of the ditch on either side more frequently, than traverse the gully beneath. The mansion being placed on the side of a hill, required but three walls, the back being dug out of the bank. This, however, made but little difference in the material, for the remaining walls were formed of tempered yellow clay, generally called *daub*, mixed with chopped straw. It was comfortably thatched, and the ridge fastened down with a sort of backbone, about four inches thick and a foot broad, of the same material as the walls. Out of this rose the wicker framework of the chimney, well plastered, both within and without. Upon the hip of the roof, to the right of the doorway, grew a luxuriant plant of house-leek, to preserve the house from fire, and the inmates from sore eyes. Upon the threshold was nailed an ass's shoe, to keep off the fairies, and preserve the milk; and on the lintel was cut a double triangle, like what the freemasons have adopted for one of their mystic signs, in order to guard the children from the evil eye; for Paddy adhered with great pertinacity to the customs of the good old times, when it was difficult to say how much of our religion was Christian and how much Pagan.

Having crossed the causeway which led over the sink or dung-pit which stood in front, and entered the cabin, the visitor would find a much neater and more comfortable residence than outward appearance would lead him to expect. Out of the back wall was dug a small shallow excavation, crossed by shelves, which served for a dresser, in which some white-staved noggins, and divers jugs, bottles, and pieces of old-fashioned crockery were displayed. To the right of the door was the domicile of the pig, with above it the roost, and a couple of odd-looking mat-work bags, with apertures in the sides for the hens to lay in. The watling couples and rafters of the roof were of a varnished jet, from long exposure to the turf smoke, setting off to advantage the wheaten straw crosses of St. Bridget* stuck here and there throughout it.

> " St. Bridget's cross hung over door,
> Which did the house from fire secure."

Around the bed, which was a fixture, was hung from the roof a thick straw matting, with a small aperture in it to gain access to the interior, over which hung a phial of holy water, and a bit of blessed palm. This was Paddy's own couch, and within it was hung his gun, and the most valuable of his fishing gear. *The room*, which was separated by the chimney and a low partition from the rest of the house, we need not enter, for all was darkness there. Throughout the small but snug dwelling were to be seen various articles expressive of the owner's more especial calling—rods, landing-nets, fish-baskets, and night-lines stowed carefully away in the roof.

Besides the "man of the house," the inmates consisted of, first, his wife, a tall, dark, strapping, " two-handed " woman, pushing for forty, or, as some said, upon the wrong side of it; but having become a mother at eighteen, she showed the wear and tear of married life more, and took less pains to conceal it, than many a spinster of fifty. It was looked upon as an event fraught with benefit to the human race, and to their immediate neighbourhood in particular, when Paddy carried off his bride; for Peggy was a Welsh too, and as a family might fairly be expected, and everybody knows that the blood of the Welshes, as well as that of the Keoghs and Cahills, beats anything living,

* Upon St. Bridget's Night, 2d February, a small cross, made of wheaten or oaten straw, of a peculiar form, which it would be impossible to describe without some pictorial representation, is made by the peasantry, and stuck somewhere in the roof, particularly in the angles and over the door. These resemble somewhat the Maltese cross. As a new *crussogue* is set up every anniversary of St. Bridget, and as they are carefully preserved, they act as an almanac to tell the age of the house. The lines we have quoted are from the old poem of " Hesperi Neso-Graphia," printed in 1791.

except that of a black cat's tail or his lug, for the cure of the wild-fire, the gossips hoped that a Welsh, by father and mother, would soon be able to eradicate the disease from the whole country side.*

The result of this marriage was a son and a daughter, the former of whom, partaking of the dark complexion, and tall, slight figure of the mother, was now a handsome youth, just stretching into manhood; the latter, who took after the father, was a year younger than her brother. As Paddy was not much at home, but lived chiefly by the river side, or among the houses of the neighbouring gentry, his son Michael—or Michauleen,† as he used to be called when a boy—generally looked after the affairs of the little farm, but occasionally accompanied the father upon his piscatorial excursions, particularly when the May-fly was out in early summer, and Paddy required an assistant at the cross-line.‡ The boy was of rather a romantic turn—quiet, taciturn, and thoughtful—much given to fairy lore, of which both father and mother possessed not only a plentiful stock, but peculiar powers of narration. There was not a rath nor forth in the whole country side but Michael knew the legend of it. He believed in the good people, and the leprehauns, and pookas, and banshees, and thivishes or fetches, with as unwavering a faith as he did in Father Crump's power to turn a man's hair grey, or twist his head on his shoulders, or old Friar Geoghegan's ability to wallop the devil out of a madman with

* This is one of the most widely-spread superstitions in Ireland. Cutaneous erysipelas is known to the people under the various names of the rose, wildfire, St. Anthony's fire, *tene fiadh*, the sacred fire, or *tinne Diadh*, God's fire, the *sacer ignis* of ancient authors; and is believed to be cured by the means specified in the text, or by having the part rubbed with a wedding-ring, or even a gold ring of any description. There is another form of this malady, of a more fatal nature, which is believed to be the result of a blast, and is called the *fiolun*, or *fellon*, for the cure of which some extraordinary practices are still in vogue. These we shall describe on another occasion.

† Michel, Micheleen, or Michauleen, Mickey, Myke, and Michaul, are all synonyms for Michael.

‡ This method of fishing is used with a natural fly, the *libellula*, or green drake, with murderous effect, upon the flat, calm pools in the Suck. There are two rods employed, one on each bank, the wheel line joined in the centre; and from this depends one or more casting-lines, or droppers, about five feet long. To these are attached the flies, which, by the cross-line being kept *taut*, can be dropped with unerring precision wherever a trout is seen to rise.

a blackthorn.* Then, he knew the history of Ballintober Castle, and the story of the Well of Oran, and how, if a man lifted the sacred stone which stands beside it, all Ireland would be "drownded" in no time.

His father, though no great scholar himself, determined to have learning for his child; and many a half-crown, which Paddy got for a *bodough* trout at some of the neighbouring houses, went to Tim Dunlavy for a quarter's schooling for the little boy, who could soon not only read and write tolerably well, but had gone through the "*coorse o' Voster*" as far as "Tret and Tare;" and there is no knowing to what pitch of learning he might have arrived, nor for what sacred office he might have been prepared, had his mother had her will, and his father been more agriculturally inclined; but, as neither of these benign influences beamed upon him, he was soon obliged to relinquish such pursuits for the more profitable ones of setting potatoes and footing turf. Still his literary predilections remained, and these he indulged whenever he had an opportunity. It was one of the great inducements to young Welsh to accompany his father a-fishing, that during the dull hours of the day, from twelve till two, when "the rise" had gone off the trout, and Paddy was taking a smoke, or lying asleep on the grass till a "curl" would come on the calm waters, that he could learn off the "Battle of Aughrim, or the Fall of St. Ruth," or the "Battle of Ventry Harbour," out of one of his father's flybooks.

Young Michael was an object of special respect among the people, from the happy circumstance of his descent and birthright. A Welsh by both father and mother was not to be found everywhere, and of this the boy was rather proud; and, when even yet a child, never winced under the operation of having his thumb bound tightly with a woollen thread, and the point pricked with a needle, to extract the blood with which the afflicted person was touched.

What between the produce of the little farm, Peggy's in-

* Friar Geoghegan, whose feats in necromancy, the laying of spirits, beating of devils, and casting of charms, and other mysteries of the black art, are still well remembered in the counties of Mayo and Roscommon, was a degraded Franciscan.

dustry, and the matter of eggs and chickens, and Paddy's earnings, which, though very irregular, were often considerable, the family were well enough to live, and might, people said, have made more of themselves if all that was told of Paddy's doings was truth. It was said he had found a crock of gold in one of the towers of the old bawne of Ballintober, which was not more than a mile and a half distant from his cabin, and where Paddy and his son were often seen in the twilight, looking, they said, for moths and wall-flies among the old ivy, or bats and starlings to manufacture fishing materials; at least, so they said, but the people thought otherwise. We often endeavoured to worm the story out of the cunning angler; but, drunk or sober, he was always on his guard, and generally passed it off with a joke, or—

"Sure, Master Willie, you don't give into the likes—'tis only ould women's talk. It's myself that would be glad to own to it if I got the goold, and not be slaving myself, summer and winter, by the river's brink, as I am."

"Yes; but, Paddy, they say you made the attempt, at all events. Cannot you tell us what happened to you?"

"Oh, then, it's only all *gollymoschought*. But that's mighty fine parlimint * your honour has in the little flask; 'tis a pity it doesn't hould more, and the devil a tail we are rising to keep up our spirits."

"Come now, Paddy, since you know very well it will be quite too bright and dull these two hours to stir even a roach, let alone a trout—don't you perceive there isn't a cloud in the sky, and I can see the bottom as plain as my hand: look, even the cows have left off feeding, and are standing in the ford switching their tails to keep off the clags?—just stick the rods, and lie on your face in the grass there, and tell me all about the night you went to look after the money in the old bawne. Do, and you'll see I'll squeeze another mouthful out of the cruiskeen."

"Well, but you're mighty 'cute and disquisitive after ould stories and pishogues. I suppose I may as well be after telling it to you while the breeze is getting up; but keep an eye to the river, awourneen, and try could you see e'er a rise; and be sure

* *Parlimint*, used in contradistinction to *potteen*, or illicit whiskey.

you don't miss a gray *coughlin* or a *merrow*, if e'er a one flies past you; we'll want them coming on evening. But don't be tellin' on me, nor let on at the *big house* * that I told you the likes at all. Sure the mistress 'ud never forgive me for putting such things in your head; and maybe it's Father Crump she'd be after repatein' it to the next Sunday he dines in Dundearmot; and if she did, troth I wouldn't face him for a month of Sundays. Maybe it's to St. Ball or to St. John's Well he'd send me for my night walkin'."

"Oh, never fear, I'll keep your secret."

"Well, then, awourneen, to make a long story short, I dhramed one night that I was walking about in the *bawne*, when I looked into the old tower that's in the left hand corner, after you pass the gate, and there I saw, sure enough, a little crock, about the bigness of the bottom of a pitcher, and it full up of all kinds of money, goold, silver, and brass. When I woke next morning, I said nothin' about it, but in a few nights after I had the same dhrame over agin, ony I thought I was lookin' down from the top of the tower, and that all the flures were taken away. Peggy knew be me that I had a dhrame, for I wasn't quite asey in myself; so I ups and tells her the whole of it, when the childer had gone out. 'Well, Paddy,' says she, 'who knows but it would come thrue, and be the making of us yet; but you must wait till the dhrame comes afore you the third time, and then, sure, it can do no harm to try, anyways.' It wasn't long till I had the third dhrame, and as the moon was in the last quarter, and the nights mighty dark, Peggy put down the *grisset*,† and made a lock of

---

* The big house, or *Teach more*, is the term applied by the people to the residences of the gentry, except when they are of great extent or beauty, and then "the coort" is the word made use of. Old castles or ancient inclosures are styled *bawnes*.

† *Grisset*, a small narrow metal pan on three legs, used for melting grease, and dipping rushes in. Sometimes a fragment of an old pot is employed for the same purpose. The tongs are made red hot, and if there is no kitchen stuff at hand, a bit of fat of any kind is squeezed between the hot blades of the tongs into the grisset or its substitute, and the rushes, peeled of their outer green bark, all except one narrow stripe, are drawn through the melted grease, and laid across the stool to set. In order to permit the grease to exude with greater freedom, all the old-fashioned country pairs of tongs were made with holes in the flat of the

candles; and so, throwin' the *loy* * over my showlder, and giving Michauleen the shovel, we set out about twelve o'clock, and when we got to the castle, it was as dark that you wouldn't see your hand before you; and there wasn't a stir in the ould place, barrin' the owls that wor snorin' in the chimley. To work we went just in the middle of the flure, and cleared away the stones and the rubbish, for nearly the course of an hour, with the candles stuck in pataties, resting on some of the big stones a wan side of us. Of coorse, sorra word we said all the while, but dug and shovelled away as hard as hatters, and a mighty tough job it was to lift the flure of the same buildin'. Well, at last the loy struck on a big flag, and my heart riz within me, for I often heard tell that the crock was always covered with a flag, and so I pulled away for the bare life, and at last I got it cleared, and was just lifting the edge of it, when —— was that a trout I heard lep there abroad?"

"No, Paddy, you know very well it wasn't. Go on with your story. Didn't you see a big goat with four horns and terrible red eyes, sitting on the flag, and guarding the gold. Now tell the truth."

"Oh, what's the use in tellin' you anything about it; sure, I know by your eye you don't believe a word I am sayin'. The dickens a goat was sitting on the flag; but when both of us were trying to lift the stone, my foot slipped, and the clay and rubbish began to give way under us. 'Lord betune us and harm,' says the gossoon; and then, in the clapping of your hand, there wuz a wonderful wind rushed in through the dureway, and quinched the lights, and pitched us both down into the hole; and of all the noises you ever heard, it was about us in a minute. *M'anum san Deowl!* but I thought it was all over with us, and sorra wan of me ever thought of as much as crossin' myself; but I made out as fast as I could, and the gossoon after me, and we never stopped running 'till we stumbled over the

blades. The dipt rushes were generally kept in a piece of badger's skin, hung to the roof. Rushlights are now scarcely known, nor the sconces in which they were fixed. Pieces of tow dipped in resin are used instead.

* The *loy* was the long, narrow, one-sided spade, with an unwieldy ash handle or *feck*, the only agricultural instrument known to the bulk of the western peasants twenty years ago.

wall of the big intrance, and it was well we didn't go clane into the moat. Troth, you wouldn't give three haypence for me when I was standin' in the road—the *bouchal* itself was stouter—with the wakeness that came over me. *Och, millia murdher!* I wasn't the same man for many a long day; but that was nawthin' to the turmintin' I got from every body about findin' the goold, for the shovel that we left after us was dishcovered, and there used to be daelers and gintlemin from Dublin,—antitrarians, I think they call them,--comin' to the house continually, and axin' Peggy for some of the coins we found in the ould castle.

" There now, you have the whole of it—wet the landin'-net agra, and run after that beautiful green-drake that's just gone over us, while I see whether there is anything left in the bottle."

The popular opinions with respect to hidden treasure are, that they are generally under the guardianship of spirits, who assume various hideous shapes to affright mortals who seek to discover them. Sometimes the good people interfere, and some of their special favourites are, under their guidance and permission, enabled to obtain possession of the hidden gold; but it is strictly imposed upon those to whom the secret is revealed, either in the form of a dream or as a direct revelation, that they must seek the treasure at a particular time, not utter a word during the search, and keep the secret of its discovery for seven years after. Several of the great lake serpents and water-cows of our Irish Fairy Mythology are supposed to guard treasures; in some instances black cats are similarly employed.

The ruins of Ballintober Castle are amongst the most magnificent in Connaught, and are memorable as the last stronghold of the O'Conors. The castle, which stands on an elevated ridge by the road-side, above the little village of Ballintober, four miles from the town of Castlebar, consists of a quadrangular inclosure, 270 feet in length, and 230 feet in breadth,* with

* See an account of this castle in " Weld's Statistical Survey of the County Roscommon;" also views of it in the book styled " Grose's Antiquities;" consult

four flanking towers, and one upon each side of the great entrance, the whole surrounded by a deep fosse, portions of which still retain water. Mr. Weld has remarked upon the strong resemblance which the towers of this castle bear to some of those in Wales. "No one tower, it is true," he says, "is comparable to the Eagle Tower at Caernarvon. Nevertheless, the south-west tower at Ballintober is a superb piece of architecture, and, for its general effect, amongst the most imposing remains of antiquity that I can call to recollection in Ireland." There are two localities of this name in Connaught—Baile-an-tobhair-Phaidraig, the town of the Well of St. Patrick, in Mayo, and Baile-an-tobhair-Brighde, that of St. Bridget, now under consideration. This place is, among other things, memorable as the birth-place of the celebrated Cathal Crovederg, or "Charles the Red-Handed," the illegitimate son of Turlough-More O'Conor, the brother of Roderick, and last of the Irish monarchs. About this prince, who was born in the latter end of the twelfth century,—and who, says the Ulster Annals, was " the best Irishman, from the time of Brien Boroma, for gentility and honour; the upholder, mighty and puissant, of the country; keeper of peace; rich and excellent,"—there are many romantic tales and superstitious legends, still lingering with the people in the vicinity, which, were they woven into a novel, would far surpass most modern works of fiction. When we have a novelist not only acquainted with Irish history and antiquities, but possessing the power of fusing the ancient legend with the drama of modern life and impulse; making the feelings that influence the lover or the hero subservient to the chronicle; picturing the past, through the knowledge of the human heart at the present—then, and then only will Irish history be known and appreciated. Cathal of the Red Hand was the son of a beautiful girl of very small stature, named Gearrog Ny-Moran, of the Muhall territory. When the queen heard what had occurred, she, like Sarah of old, commenced a bitter perse-

"The Annals of the Four Masters," A.D. 1312, *et seq.* It is said to have been erected in the time of King John. The north-western tower was repaired or rebuilt in 1684. The south-western tower, that alluded to in the text, is in a state of great dilapidation; but the present proprietor, H. Packenham Mahon, Esq., is, at the instance of the author, about to have it repaired.

cution against the king's mistress, and had, as was customary at the time, recourse to witchcraft and sorcery to prolong the sufferings of the unhappy maiden. Like Juno, before the birth of Hercules, she, with the assistance of a noted witch, set a charm, consisting of a bundle of elder rods, tied with a magic string, knotted with nine knots. This she hung up in her chamber, and watched with great care. Stratagem, however, achieved what humanity could not induce. The queen, while walking on the terrace, was accosted by a female (the midwife disguised), who entreated alms for a poor woman who had just been confined in the neighbouring village. On hearing who it was, she was so enraged, that she instantly rushed to her apartment, and cut the charm into pieces. The spell was broken, and the bond-woman's child was born. For several years after, Gearrog and her son were protected from the jealous fury of the queen by the people; and both were long harboured in the monasteries of Connaught. As time wore on, however, the Church was insufficient against the wrath of the offended queen, and Cathal * was obliged to fly to a distant province, where, in the garb of a peasant, he supported himself by manual labour. At length the King of Connaught died; and the people declared they would have no monarch but his son, Cathal Crovederg, if he could be found. Heralds were sent forth, and proclamations issued, according to the fashion of the times, yet still no tidings of the elected king. One day, as harvest was drawing to its close, a *Boll-scaire*, or herald, from the Court of Ballintober, entered a field in Leinster, where some of the peasantry were at work reaping rye, and told the oft-repeated tale of the missing monarch of Connaught. Cathal, who was among the reapers, heard the story, and stood for some minutes lost in reverie. He then, removing the cover with which he always concealed the mark, held up the red hand, and throwing down the reaping-hook, exclaimed—"*Slan leath a corrain anois do'n cloideam*"—*i. e.*, Farewell, sickle; now for the sword! The Bollscaire recognizing him, both he, and the men who were along with him in the field, prostrated themselves before him, and proclaimed him

* For the cause of his cognomen of Red Hand, see "The Annals of the Four Masters," A.D. 1224.

King of Connaught.   He was afterwards crowned at Carnfree, near Tulsk, by the chieftains and the coorbs of Sil-Murray, and "Cathal's Farewell to the Rye" is a proverb and an air still well known in Roscommon and Galway.*

In the southern wall, which is only divided by a moat from the adjoining road, there are a number of large oval apertures, which, from their being nearly closed with ivy of immense growth, look, at first view, like windows.   Such, however, they were not.   Their history is well known to a few of the old people in the neighbourhood, and is connected with a circumstance so little known that we cannot forbear relating it here.

About the end of last century, the family of O'Conor *Donn*, or *Dun*, the lineal descendants of the Connaught monarchs, consisted of Dominick O'Conor, of Clonalis, who lived in princely style, and his brothers Thomas and Alexander, besides some females.   In the year 1786, a will, said to have been made by Hugh O'Connor, an ancestor of this line, was discovered accidentally between the leaves of a card-table, which had been screwed together for a great number of years, and had lain among the effects of the late Lord Athenry.   This document, from which it appeared that the castle and estate of Ballintober, which had long before passed from the O'Conor family, had not been included in the original confiscation of their estates, by some means found its way into the hands of Alexander O'Conor, a man of very eccentric habits, and not over-strong mental capacity, who resided in a poor cabin at a village called Creglaghan, who was till the day of his death, which took place at a very advanced age, called by the people "Masther Sandy."   This man, though dressed little better than a peasant, and living in the fashion which we have described, was looked up to by the people as a prince of the

* Among the curious memorabilia of Connaught is a book styled "Recollections of Skiffington Gibbon, from 1796 to the present year, 1829," in which most of the scandal and gossip of the county Roscommon is set forth.   This man was originally a "shop boy" in Castlerea, and afterwards traversed the country and levied black mail on all the nobility and gentry around; threatening to expose to light the skeleton in each family who did not contribute to his support.   The tale of "Garnege Nevoran" is therein repeated as we often heard it when a boy at Ballintober Castle.

royal line of Roderick, the last monarch of Ireland, and he was certainly descended from Cathal Crovederg, his son. Sandy determined to profit by the circumstance of the will; and taking advantage of the lawless and disturbed condition of the country at the time, and his remote position from the seat of government and power, collected in a few days an army—if such a term can be applied to an undisciplined armed mob—and took possession of Ballintober Castle, which he commenced to fortify, and even procured one or two cannon, which he placed at the entrance. They drove the neighbouring cattle within the inclosure, set up a still-house, gave the "hoight of good living" to all the pipers and fiddlers that came to them, and ate, drank, danced, and caroused, for some weeks, until the attention of the government was directed to the circumstance by the matter being discussed in the Irish House of Commons, when troops and a park of artillery were sent down to dislodge the insurgent chief. Upon the news of their approach, O'Conor and his followers immediately fled; but the army having arrived within cannon shot of the castle, and seeing it deserted, fired some shots at it from the neighbouring eminence of Ballyfinnegan hill. It was these shots which made the apertures to which we have alluded.*

The spring of 1823 had passed by, and with the early summer appeared a partial outbreak of the Irish fever, which annually bursts into a flame about May or June. Paddy Welsh was one of its first victims. He went out, as usual, to wet his rod in one of the neighbouring brooks, then swollen with a recent night's rain; but he soon had to return, with a shivering and a pain in his back, which he well knew foreboded "the sickness." For a few days he endeavoured to shake it off; but without effect. Cures of various kinds were had recourse to, to avert the impending fever. One of his neighbours, a mighty knowledgable woman, scraped some clay

* The writer of this article remembers, when a child, hearing Alexander O'Conor give an account of his seizure of Ballintober, and has often conversed with persons who witnessed the progress of the rebel army from Creglaghan to the old castle. See the *Gentleman's Magazine* for February 1786, and the Journals of the Irish House of Commons of that date. See also an account of the transaction in the *Dublin University Magazine* for July 1840, p. 9.

from the floor just within the threshold, because it was hallowed by the frequently repeated " *Go mannee Dia in Sho,*" "God save all here," pronounced over it, as the foot of the stranger trod it on entering the house; and heating it in a skillet, she put it into the leg of a coarse worsted stocking, and applied it to the small of his back. It was of no avail: he had to take to his bed, from which he never arose. The fifteenth day saw him a corpse—his wife a widow—his children orphans. He was waked and buried with all due honour and solemnity; and, more than that, he was lamented by ourselves and others many a long day. Peace to his ashes! He was one of the quaintest companions, and the most astute fisherman that frequented the banks of the Suck for many a long year; and should any of our angling friends ever visit the locality we have described, and inquire after *Paudeen Brannagh*, they will hear a recital of fishing wonders and exploits such as modern scepticism might be unwilling to receive. During our own boyhood, when watching his practised hand throwing a red-tackle, or a black-and-orange, over the very nose of a trout, under an impending bank on the opposite brink of the river, with his light whip-rod springing from the very wheel, and at least five-and-thirty yards of line out—or listening with gaping avidity to the doctrines he enunciated, as he stood upon his longer leg, supporting himself with the handle of the landing-net, complacently viewing our efforts to imitate his casting—or when leaning over the back of the chair whereon he sat, with his feathers and silks, and various-coloured dubbings, and bits of skins, and the numerous *materiel* for manufacturing his flies, on the little table before him, in the door-way of his snug cabin, and heard him descant upon their several virtues, and how each was obtained, we regarded him with reverence approaching to awe. As he took up each bit of dressing he descanted on its virtues, and told how he scaled a high demesne-wall, at the risk of his neck, to get the topping of that golden pheasant, and took a hackling excursion all the ways to Carlow, to get that jay's wing—robbed a church-steeple of its community of starlings for their feathers—how he stole that bit of macau out of the tail of a showman's bird while he kept him engaged in conversation—how he learned the secret of dying pig's-down from a travelling tinker, and of tempering hooks, by shaking them in a leather bag over the fire, like the Limerick O'Shaughnessy—all this we say, together with the inexhaustible fund of legend, song, and superstition, which he possessed, made us, from a very early period, look up to him with admiration; and we greatly fear that the remembrance of these days would induce us to linger in the company of our old friend and preceptor longer than our readers—if not brothers of the gentle craft—might be willing to listen to us.

———

The summer had glided imperceptibly into autumn, and the great bulk of the crop having been gathered in, and the long nights and short days of early winter approaching with unusual rapidity, the time was propitious for those who stir up rebellion among the people to ply their special craft; and ribbonism, such as that we have alluded to in the commencement of this chapter, soon sank deep and spread wide throughout the peasant and small-farmer class of the hitherto peaceful barony of Ballintober. Those who took no part in the night-walkings, or secret meetings, were compelled to contribute a sort of black mail for the furtherance of "the cause;" and wherever a gun, or any description of fire-arms, or any sort of weapon, was known to exist, thither a nocturnal visit was made, and the inmates of the houses were compelled to deliver it up, and got soundly thrashed if they did not do so with alacrity.

Hitherto the ribbonmen and their captains had, partly in remembrance of the many kindly offices rendered to them by our former acquaintance, the fisherman—the lively planxties he had played at their weddings, or the droll humour he had shown at their mothers' wakes, with what effect he repeated the rosary as their fathers' corpses were carried three times round the grave-yard of Baslick, and what a world of money he had gathered at the gentlemen's houses when he acted Beel-zebub in the Christmas mummers, and how many a hook he had mounted for them when they went, of a Sunday morning, a-fishing for perch in the deep still pools of the Lara; or, perhaps, respecting the grief of the wife and orphans—they had left the Widow Welsh's house undisturbed, although it was well known that the old French fusee, with the velvet-and-silver-mounted cheek-piece, "to make it kick asey," was still in the cabin, and that Michael was now of age to take part in the councils as well as the standing army of the country. But as the disturbance and the disaffection spread wider in the neighbouring districts of Mayo and Galway, men appeared at the lodges and marshalled the people, who were strangers to the feelings we have alluded to, and paid no respect to either "widdies or orphants."

After his father's death, young Welsh's natural thoughtfulness and reserve seemed rather to increase. He appeared more wrapt within himself, was more than ever given to reading, and to wandering alone by the old forts, through the ruined castles, and by the ancient grave-yards in the neighbourhood. Still, this in no wise interfered with his daily work. He had clamped the turf, and pitted the potatoes, and stacked the lock of corn, and was mending the thatch with as much, if not greater, energy than before. Neither were his family affections in any degree weakened by his peculiar state of mind. He was as dutiful to his mother and as affectionate to his sister Biddy as ever, but still it was evident that he was not as hearty as in days gone by. Men of such like temperament feel any sudden mental shock, or any great violence done to the affections, more than persons of greater vivacity of disposition; for, although they do not exhibit the same active show of grief, it invariably sinks deeper in their souls, and remains longer graven into their memory, while they want that power of resilience within themselves to shake off their despondency; and, being from habit unaccustomed to society, they are consequently unable to take advantage of that influence which it, along with the soothing effects of time, generally exerts in assuaging sorrow.

The death of his parent had evidently preyed on the young man; his favourite haunts, during the long summer evenings

just past, had been among the ruins of the old bawne, where he
so often went in earlier times, with his father, to catch moths
and look out for wall-flies; or he lingered by the river's banks
(although he never fished) to watch the large evening trout, as,
with deep sullen plunge, it roved through the still deep pools
in quest of prey, and to listen to the well-known sound of the
heavy fish, as, without splash and scarcely with any noise, it
sucked down the gnats and night-flies from the surface, in the
dark shadows of the overhanging bushes, while the wide-
spreading circles from the broken water spread out, and inter-
sected each other in all directions, as if oil had been dropped
upon the limpid bosom of the stream. Here he would sit or walk
during the still calm hours before moonlight, after the light
laughing gulls (*gula ridens*) had skimmed gently and gracefully
over the meadows—when the bat wheeled and circled over his
head, and the corn-craik had commenced its nightly serenade—
long after the cuckoo had got hoarse with mocking, and the
only discordant sound was the night owl's shriek, as it flapped
its light feathery wings in noiseless flight along the hedgerows.
The not unfragrant smell of the *baton*, or burning land in the
distance, mingled with the perfume of the meadow-sweet; and,
now and then, the sharp, interrupted bark of the colley in the
far off village, came echoless upon the ear over the broad flat
pastures of the surrounding country. What his musings were
we know not—companions he had but few—friends, such friends
as one opens their heart to in these balmy hours of witching
eve, he had none.   With the exception of his mother and sister,
he was alone—yes, alone in the world; but he knew it not, he
felt it not; it was the result of the peculiar temper of the mind
within him—the circumstances in which he was placed—all the
external surroundings of the man.

If he passed the cross roads during the dance of a Sunday
evening, he rested without any shyness for a while among the
crowd, and kindly, if not cordially, returned the greetings of
his neighbours; and if some sprightly lass stepped up to him,
and, curtseying before him, said, " Michel, agra, I am dancin'
to you," the pale, dark-haired youth did not refuse the offered
hand; he danced, and did it well, and gave the piper a penny,

and his partner, if she were willing, a *goithera*,* and share of a naggin. But the moment he got an opportunity he slipped away, and the people said, " Poor boy, he takes on wonderfully since his father's death; but sure he was always in the lonesomes, and fonder of discoorsing himself than any body else."

November had come; the mornings sharp and foggy, the days bright and sunny, and the evenings cold and raw, but the middle and later hours of night so bright, that "you'd pick pins in the stubbles," when the ground became crisp with the light hoar frost. The month wore on. It was Saturday, and Mick, having finished putting the last *scollop* in the patches of thatch with which he was mending the roof, and the last *bobbin* in the *rigging*, got down off the ladder, and, about three o'clock in the afternoon, sauntered over to the bawne of Ballintober, and climbed (a favourite amusement of his) to the top of one of the highest towers of that beautiful ruin. From thence he enjoyed a most extensive prospect, over a gently undulating, but generally flat country, chiefly grass lands, with tracts of bog intervening, particularly towards the river. The landscape was interspersed with snug villages, with their long, low, drab-coloured, mud-built cabins, surrounded, however, with well-stocked haggards; and, here and there, extensive plantations of young firs and larch, distinguished by their dark green and bright yellow hues, stretching along the hill-sides from the groves of fine old timber in the adjoining valleys, marked the progress of improvement, and pointed out the residences of the wealthy country gentleman—the old English settlers, high in birth—some of the ancient Milesian stock—and the monster graziers of Roscommon; all happy compared with present times—the landlord rich, the peasant comfortable. What would we see now if we looked over the same scene ? Not one

---

* *Goithera*, a local name for a sort of soft, flat cake, made without barm, not unlike the Ulster *bap*. It is hawked about by the gingerbread seller, and itinerant confectioner, who, with a knife dipped in a mug of treacle, gives the cake an upper varnish of the sweet fluid as soon as it is purchased.

of those mansions tenanted; whole acres of that patriarchal timber felled, to supply those necessaries to the owners which they in former times dealt with liberality to their dependants, their tenants, and to the neighbouring poor; many of those houses roofless, some of them converted into poor-houses; the villages recognized only by the foundations of the cabins, and the few alder and whitethorn bushes that linger by their sites, and seem like spirits presiding over the reigning desolation; the population dead, starved, uprooted, or swept off by the pestilence; its remnant lingering away its sickly existence in the workhouse, or planted by the waters of the Ohio and the Mississippi.   But, contemplating the present aspect of the place, we are ourselves falling into the reverie in which we left the fisherman's son.

Droves of long-horned, reddish-coloured bullocks, the largest and fattest in Ireland, cropt in huge mouthfuls the deep, rank aftergrass, as if conscious that the day was passing, and that the hour of evening meal, before they were driven into the inclosure of some old castle or bare paddock for the night, was drawing near.   Large flocks of fat wethers quickly nibbled the short herbage that intervened between the recently-formed sandpits and irregular patches of dark green furze, or whins, that studded over the vast tracts of upland.   Now and then the sharp report of the fowling-piece from the margin of the bog started the snipe, which, as it rose, to change its resting-place or feeding-ground, emitted a quick, shrill cry, as of distress. Long forked trains of wild geese, high over-head, telling by their distant whistling note their great elevation, presaged a severe winter; the large grey gulls quietly sailed across in noiseless course from the Suck, to rest for the night in some of the blue *flashes* or *closhes* of water with which the country was interspersed, or to take their evening meal at the great Turlough of Carrowkeel. The golden plover uttered its shrill whistle as it coursed in low and rapid flight along the loose stone fences, and the lapwing turned up its silver under-wing to the parting daylight, as it rose in confused gambols into the still calm ether; and enormous clouds of fieldfares and starlings, almost darkening the air, appeared in the horizon, and careered, and

wheeled, and rose and fell, separated and gathered together
again, as if directed by the trumpet note of some presiding
general, who regulated their movements before they encamped
for the night; while here and there might be seen a solitary
heron, wending its noiseless way with broad expanded pinions
and outstretched legs, to roost for the night in some of the tall
fir trees in the neighbouring demesnes.

The pale, but well-defined moon, looking almost translucid
in the remaining daylight, was high in the washy sky; the
sun was settling towards the west, bright but watery; long
slanting rays of golden light shot down through broken aper-
tures in the sluggish, muddy clouds, like angels' faces peeping
through the leaden curtain that veiled the heavens, and light-
ing up with peculiar brightness the patches of red bog, or
russet potato field, on which they fell. The pale, reddish-
yellow streaking of the west, was blurred and dappled with
the vapours that exhaled from the over-saturated *curraghs* *
and swamps that stretched away towards the confines of Mayo
and Galway. The lengthened shadows of the old towers, and
even of the long curtain walls of the castle, had crossed the
still and stagnant moat, and the branching ivy, as it rustled
and waved to and fro with the evening wind, threw fantastic
shadows on the greensward of the common which surrounded
the ruin.

It was getting cold and gloomy. Michael slowly descended
by the old winding staircase, looking out from the windows of
each story as he passed down; and when he stood in the great
court, or inclosure of the castle, the gloom there appeared the
greater, from his having so lately enjoyed an extensive pros-
pect from his elevated position. The cold grey light paled in
through the long irregular apertures in the massive walls, and
the stillness was most startling. As he walked slowly and
meditatively across the court, towards the entrance leading to
his home, he suddenly stopped opposite one of the embrasures,
put his hand to his face, quickly passed it over his eyes, and
the cold drops burst forth, and stood in dew upon his face; his
heart ceased for a few moments to act, and then beat with

* *Curragh*, unreclaimed land—a sedgy, tufted, and quagmirish marsh.

quick, rapid, and irregular, but audible motion. He quailed in every member, a slight shivering passed over his frame; his lips remained apart as his jaw fell, and a choking feeling of want of air seized him by the throat—it was with difficulty he could maintain his standing. Still, there he gazed—his eyes set, but riveted on the fringed opening in the wall. He took off his hat, raised his right hand, and devoutly crossed himself on the forehead, shoulders, and breast. His lips moved, but he uttered no audible sound as he inwardly repeated the usual invocation to the Trinity; he approached the situation of the object of his terror, and walked again slowly backwards, still keeping his eyes fixed on the spot. At last the noise of some sheep clattering over a loose part of the wall, diverted his attention; and when he looked again, his breath came more freely. The sight of the shepherd and his dog, now following the sheep, seemed to nerve him sufficiently to leave the spot, and he hurried homeward, downcast and unstrung.

Evidently something appeared to him, either in reality or in imagination, which had given no ordinary shock to his nervous system. His face was ghastly pale, and its expression was that of one who had suffered intense pain ; and the suffering, though but for a few minutes, had left its traces still deeply lined into his countenance. The lips—those uncontrollable dial-plates of the mind—yet quivered, though they were compressed until the blood had almost left them. The lip's emotion is unmanageable—no actor can imitate it. The angles of the mouth were drawn slightly downward; the forehead deeply seamed; the eyes were wild, and did not appear to move in unison ; the voice, as he returned the salutation of a neighbour in crossing the moat, was hollow and slightly tremulous ; and his limbs moved quickly, but rather irregularly. Every now and then he gulped, as if swallowing large draughts of air; and as he proceeded homewards, sometimes slowly, and then almost at a run, he occasionally turned sharply round, as if to see whether there was not some one following him. At each angle of the road, at every tree, he stopped to examine; and he carefully tried to avoid the few persons that happened to be in his path, until he got to the *boreen* leading to his house. Here, at the end of the lane, he rested, and leaning his back against the ditch, endeavoured to compose himself, and arrange his features for the meeting with his family, for he was himself conscious that some great change must have passed over him; and as he walked up the lane a deep sigh escaped him, and he exclaimed aloud—"Oh, Queen of Heaven! what will become of my poor mother and Biddy?"

It was almost dark as young Welsh "drew over" a stool, and sat moodily looking into the fire at his mother's hearth. She plied her wheel without remark, and his sister was busily engaged in straining the potatoes on the *skeib* for their evening meal. Neither of them remarked anything unusual in his manners or appearance, and his custom of passing in and out without exchanging a word had nothing novel in it. "The little girl" placed the table opposite the fire, and put a rushlight in the long wooden sconce beside it, and then laid down the *murpheys* and the drop of milk in the noggin,—for it is not unusual for all the members of a small Irish peasant family to drink out of the same vessel, although each apportions a certain part of the brim to their special use. The mother pushed her wheel to one side, drew near the table, and looking at the haggard face of her son, uttered a suppressed scream, and exclaimed:—

"Saints in Heaven! Michauleen, jewel, what's come over you at all at all? Does anything ail you, *mu lannou bocht?* You look as if you'd seen what was n't right."

"Troth, then, mother dear, you are not far from it; I'll never be the same man again—it's all over with me."

Peggy threw her arms round her brother, and, while the big sobs burst from her, she entreated him to tell them what had happened to him, or whether anybody had vexed him.

"Oh, no, the sorra vex. I'm neither sick, sore, nor sorry, for the matter of that; but I know I'm done for, any-how,—and 'tis n't for my own sake I care, but to be after lavin' you and my mother all alone, and without any one to look after ye. Mother," said he, gazing steadily upon the pale anxious face that was bent upon him, "I've seen the *thivish*. I stud

face to face with my fetch this blessed evening, straight for-
ninst me in the bawne of Ballintober. There it was in the gap
in the ould wall, as like me as if I stud before a lookin'-glass.
Whatever I did, it did the same; and I thought it might be
one of the boys making game of me, till I blessed myself—but
it never riz a hand, and then I knew it was the *thivish*. It
was well I did n't *fall out of my standing*. Mother, I 'm a gone
man, and I thought as much this many a day." And the swim-
ming eyes refused longer to hold the scalding fluid which now
ran down his care-worn cheeks.

The family were silent for some minutes, awe-struck by the
sad warning, in which they all more or less believed. At last
the mother said:—

" Michauleen, *sthore ma chree* that you were, never mind
it; don't give in to the likes. I often heard tell of people that
saw fetches, and never a hurt came on them."

" Thrue for you, mother, but that was in the morning; or
maybe it was some one else's fetch they saw."

Still, though she endeavoured to calm his fears, it was
evident, from the anxious countenance with which she fre-
quently regarded him, that the loving mother's mind was not
at rest upon the subject; but she struggled to suppress, if she
could not quite conceal her agitation, and strove to direct his
attention to other matters. At length she persuaded him to
take a drop of sperrits in a warm drink, and to go to bed, as she
was sure some sickness was over him.

The night fell dark and windy; the stars were but transi-
torily revealed as the dark masses of clouds passed under them;
and by ten or eleven o'clock the whole country seemed locked
in deep repose—the dogs being carefully housed, and the
lights extinguished in every homestead. To suppose, how-
ever, from this that tranquillity prevailed, would be a great
mistake.

So long as the peace of the country rested with the magis-
trates, barony constables, and local civil corps, there was no

general rising of the ribbonmen; but the new police, or Peelers, had just entered Connaught, and a party of six and a sergeant having been then located in the village of Ballintober, it was considered an aggression on the liberty of the subject, with which the suspension of the Habeas Corpus Act could bear no comparison. It was accordingly arranged, in ribbon conclave, that the police-barrack should be attacked upon this very night, and its inmates put to the pike or the fire. For this purpose, reinforcements from the ribbonmen of distant parts of the neighbouring counties were to meet those of the vicinity in a field called the Stone Park, not far from the old castle. One of these parties—that from the county Galway—passing over the ford of the Suck, just opposite Welsh's cabin, and not being influenced by any feelings of sympathy towards the widow and her melancholy son, knocked at the door, and awaking up the inmates, not only took possession of the old fusee, but peremptorily demanded the attendance of Michael upon their midnight excursion.

As we advance towards the climax and catastrophe of this tale, the simple truth presses stronger upon us than any imaginative description we could give, although " founded upon fact." We have, therefore, no desire to linger at this part of our narrative for the purpose of describing the mother's entreaties and the sister's agony, as this poor young man was hurried from his quiet home by lawless ruffians, with whose faces none of the inmates of that sequestered spot were acquainted. It is unnecessary to recite the deep blasphemous execrations, the harsh menace, the rough usage, or coarse ribald jokes with which the females were assailed, as Michael Welsh was forcibly decorated with the insignia of a ribbonman on his own floor.

Upon the spot specified were collected several hundred ribbonmen, armed with every description of missile or weapon that was possible to procure—old rusty fire-arms, several of which would not go off, and if they did, it would be with greater danger to the person who held them than to those against whom they were pointed—bayonets on the tops of poles, scythe-blades fastened into stout sticks, pitchforks, a few old swords and halberts, and a trifle of pikes remaining over since '98. Even those who could not procure such weapons had armed themselves with stout alpeens, and all bore more or less about them the badges of that lawless society. Some oaths were administered to the hitherto uninitiated; but the direct purpose of their assembling was known only to the leaders. The wavering, the young, and the timid—and among these Michael Welsh—were placed in the centre; and the party moved on silently towards the neighbouring village.

The police, as is generally the case on all such occasions, had timely intimation of their intended visit. The barrack was a thatched cabin, and, consequently, not tenable for a moment after it was set on fire. The police-serjeant, an old Waterloo man, named Greenfield, who was afterwards an officer in the London police, was not long in coming to a decision as to the course he should pursue for the safety of himself and his men. To remain where he was, was death—to retreat into some of the neighbouring towns he thought dishonourable: so he at once evacuated his barrack, and, during the darkness of the night, retreated into the neighbouring ruin—the old bawne of Ballintober. Here he distributed his six men in two of the apertures which we have described in the south-western wall of the old castle. The night was particularly dark, and the great depth of the wall, as well as the surrounding ivy, would have completely concealed them, even had the night been one of bright moonlight. The road leading toward the barrack lay along this wall, but separated from it by the castle moat, a deep trench with water at least four feet deep. When they had remained here about two hours, their attention was attracted to the irregular tread of the approaching multitude. On they came in silence; their white shirts and ribboned hats visible even through the darkness. When about a third of the party had passed, the police fired into the throng from their place of concealment. It was unnecessary to repeat the volley: a panic seized the multitude, who, throwing aside their arms, rushed in tumultuous terror wherever a means of escape opened. In a very few minutes the road was as quiet and as unoccupied as it had been half-an-hour before. Several groans were heard from the wounded or the dying, who were carried off by their friends. The police remained still within their entrenched fort; and two of the party were sent off across the fields into the neighbouring town of Castlerea, for the large police force stationed there at that time.

The grey of the morning gave sufficient light to distinguish the surrounding objects, as the magistrates and a large body of police arrived on the spot. Upon the road lay on its back the dead body of a young man, cold and stiff; the upturned face calm as that of those whose death has been sudden and immediate; the white shirt, which was worn outside the clothes, dabbled with blood, and soiled with the heavy foot-marks of the mob who must have passed over the body in their flight. Upon examination it was found that two balls had entered the chest. The body was that of Michael Welsh. Around it lay, scattered on all sides, the weapons which had been thrown down. More than a dozen decorated hats, and several shoes, also lay about; and traces of blood were discernible in several places besides that occupied by the corpse. A low wall, which formed the road boundary on the side opposite to the moat, was levelled for about twenty yards, such was the impetuosity with which the multitude had rushed head-long on every side, in escaping from the deadly fire.*

During the day the body of the unfortunate man was placed in a cart, along with the ribbon insignia found upon the road, and carried to the county town, where a meeting of magistrates was immediately held, under the direction of the militia major to whom we have already alluded, and who then commanded the district.

There was but a small gathering at the chapel of Ballintober upon that Sunday; the great majority of the peasantry had either fled or were in concealment. A panic and a gloom seemed to have entered into the hearts of all; and good old Father Crump's exhortation from the altar, after mass, upon the virtues of peace and quietness—for he was too mild and too

---

* More persons than Michael Welsh were shot that night; two died of their wounds subsequently. A medical man, a near relative of the writer's, attended some of the wounded; they were not natives of the vicinity, but had come from a great distance in the County Galway.

good to denounce any one—was addressed to women and the few old people from the immediate vicinity.

*   *   *   *   *   *   *

The old gaol of Roscommon stood, and, although now converted to other purposes, still stands, in the market-place, in the centre of the town. It is an exceedingly high, dark, gloomy-looking building, with a castellated top, like one of the ancient fortresses that tower above the houses in many of the continental cities. It can be discerned at a great distance ; and, taken in connexion with the extensive ruins of O'Conor's Castle, in the suburbs, and the beautiful abbey upon the other side of the town, seems to partake of the character of the middle-age architecture. The fatal drop was, perhaps, the highest in Ireland. It consisted of a small doorway in the front of the third story, with a simple iron beam and pulley above, and the *lapboard* merely a horizontal door hinged to the wall beneath, and raised or let fall by means of a sliding-bolt, which shot from the wall when there was occasion to put the apparatus of death in requisition.

Fearful as this elevated gallows appeared, and unique in its character, it was not more so than the finisher of the law who then generally officiated upon it. No decrepid wretch, no crime-hardened ruffian, no secret and mysterious personage, who was produced occasionally disguised and masked, plied his dreadful trade here. Who, think you, *gentle* reader—who now, perhaps, recoils from these unpleasant but truthful minutiæ— officiated upon this gallows high?—a female!—a middle-aged, stout-made, dark-eyed, swarthy-complexioned, but by no means forbidding-looking woman—the celebrated Lady Betty—the finisheress of the law—the unflinching priestess of the executive for the Connaught circuit, and Roscommon in particular, for many years. Few children, born or reared in that county thirty, or even five-and-twenty, years ago, who were not occasionally frightened into "being good," and going to sleep, and not crying when left alone in the dark, by *huggath a' Pooka*, or, "here's Lady Betty."

The only fragment of her history which we have been able to collect is, that she was a person of violent temper, though in manners rather above the common, and possessing some education. It was said that she was a native of the County Kerry, and that by her harsh usage she drove her only son from her at an early age. He enlisted; but, in course of years, returned with some money in his pocket, the result of his campaigning. He knocked at his father's door, and asked a night's lodging, determined to see for himself whether the brutal mother he had left had in any way repented, or was softened in her disposition before he would reveal himself. He was admitted, but not recognized. The mother, discovering that he possessed some money, murdered him during the night. The crime was discovered, and the wretched woman sentenced to be hanged, along with the usual dockful of sheep-stealers, whiteboys, shop-lifters, and cattle-houghers, who, to the amount of seven or eight at a time, were invariably " turned off" within four-and-twenty hours after their sentences at each assizes. No executioner being at hand, time pressing, and the sheriff and his deputy being men of refinement, education, humanity, and sensibility, who could not be expected to fulfil the office which they had undertaken,—and for which one of them, at least, was paid,—this wretched woman, being the only person in the gaol who could be found to perform the office, consented; and under the name of Lady Betty, officiated, unmasked and undisguised, as *hangwoman* for a great number of years after; and she used also to flog publicly in the streets, as a part of her trade.* Numerous are the tales related of her exploits, which we have now no desire to dwell upon. We may, however, mention one extraordinary trait of her character. She was in the habit of drawing, with a burnt stick, upon the walls of her apartment, portraits of all the persons she executed.

Before daybreak, upon the Monday morning after Michael Welsh was shot, several labourers, surrounded by a guard of police, might be seen erecting two tall scaffolding poles in the market-square, opposite the gaol. When this was completed, the cart containing the body of the fisherman's son, with the redoubted Lady Betty sitting in it, emerged from the back

* This history of Lady Betty we have received from persons who were perfectly acquainted with her during her long residence in Roscommon.

entrance of the gaol; and, having reached the gibbet, the body, with the assistance of some of the gaol officials, was hoisted by her ladyship to the top of the poles, which stood about six or eight feet apart; and from these the body was suspended by the hands, in that attitude which nations are accustomed to adore!! Upon the head was tied one of the decorated hats, on which was pasted a placard with the word "RIBBONMAN" written upon it. The breast was bare—the wounds exposed. When the day broke, the inhabitants of Roscommon had this horrid spectacle before their eyes, placed there by order of the governor of the district.

The rain soon came down in torrents, and continued to pour all day. Every spout and eave-course gave forth its rill; the dirty streets ran seas of mud which flashed in long undulations over the flag-way or pavement when set in motion by the passing vehicle; several of the shops remained closed, and few of the respectable classes were to be seen in the streets; old ladies took to their beds, and young ones made preparations for a hasty departure to the metropolis; reports of the most exaggerated description were circulated upon all sides, and large bodies of military arriving from Athlone and Galway, strengthened the apprehensions of the timid, and confirmed the reports of the alarmists. The magistrates met in conclave all day, and it was expected that something wonderful was to take place next morning.

Around the gibbet stood a guard of military and police, and upon one of the kerb-stones of the adjoining street sat two females, who occasionally uttered the wildest strains of grief that the Irish cry, particularly when uttered by those in the position of the mother and sister of the gibbeted corpse, is capable of expressing.

During the night the rain cleared off; towards morning a smart frost set in, and after it, the sun rose large, red, and blushing through the misty air; but soon the fog cleared off, and the same brightness which shines equally on the just and the unjust lit up the old castles, and gaols, and abbeys, and houses, and threw its slanting rays through the open doorways of the long, low cabins, and evoked a reeking steam from all the dunghills in the dirty lanes of Roscommon. Hundreds of the peasantry might be seen approaching the town from all directions. Magistrates and country gentlemen, armed to the teeth, with the light frost hanging in whitish spray upon their hair and whiskers, and clouds of vapour steaming from every mouth and nostril, arrived in gigs and tax-carts. Some great spectacle, of which a rumour had gone abroad, was evidently expected. Towards noon the town was thronged with people; every window was occupied; many climbed to the house-tops; wherever footing or elevation was to be obtained, thither crowded some of the anxious throng. There was no ribald jesting— even neighbours scarcely exchanged a greeting; sullen anger, fierce determination, savage revenge, brooded over the mass, and was fearfully depicted in every face. If we said that from twenty to thirty thousand people filled the streets of Roscommon that day we should not exaggerate. That beautiful regiment of dragoons, " The Green Horse," with their bright helmets and flourishing horsetails, paraded the streets, and parties of foot soldiers and police took up positions in different parts of the town, the sun glancing brightly from their polished firelocks.

About noon, the gibbeted body was taken down, placed in a sitting position in a cart, the arms extended, and tied to pitchforks, the back supported by a plank; around the body were arranged, as in an arm-trophy, the various guns, and pikes, and scythes, and other weapons, which had been taken from the ribbonmen for some time past; and on several of those were placed the hats picked up on the battle-field of Ballintober. This sad spectacle led the procession; after it, advanced slowly three horses and cars, and to the tail-board of each cart was bound a man, naked to the waist, who had been sentenced to be flogged three times through the towns of Roscommon, Strokestown, and Castlerea, but the execution of whose sentence had, until then, been deferred, in the hope that the country would have remained quiet. Lady Betty, for some reason, did not officiate upon this occasion. One of the men was flogged by a Sicilian boy—the others, by drummers belonging to regiments then in the province.

The military lined the streets; the procession moved through the long straggling town. The rere was brought up by a cavalcade of magistrates, chiefly on horseback; in the centre of this part of the procession rolled slowly on, to "flogging pace," an open chariot, in which sat the Major, who ordered and directed the proceedings—we have no desire to describe him—and by his side lolled a large, unwieldy person, with bloated face and slavering lip—the ruler of Connaught, the sheriff at George Robert Fitzgerald's execution—the great gauger-maker of the west—*The* Right Honourable.

Let us drop the curtain. If this was not Connaught, it was Hell.

We have only to remark that the scene, with all its horrors, would have been repeated in two of the other towns of the county, but for petitions to government from some of their inhabitants.

Well—it was a frightful spectacle, horrifying and demoralizing, but perhaps applicable to the time and circumstances; at all events, it completely put an end to ribbonism in that district for many a year.

CHAPTER IV.

" We let mischievous witches with their charms,
    We let hobgoblins, fairies, whose sense we see not,
    Fray us into things that be not."
                                SPENCER.

FAIRY ARCHÆOLOGY AND MEDICO-RELIGIOUS CEREMONIES.

The Blast—Story of John Fitzjames—Cleena and the Fairy-Woman—The Dedication — The Meal Cure — The Fallen Angels — Mac Coise's Swan — Mary Kelly's Abduction — The Grave Watchers, a Legend of Fin Varrah, and Knockmah—The Fairy Nurse : a Tale of Innis-Shark.

THE fairies, or "good people"—the *dhoine shee* of the northerns—are looked upon by us from beyond the Shannon, as the great agents and prime movers in all accidents, diseases, and death, in "man or baste;" causing the healthfulness and fertility of seasons, persons, cattle, and localities; blighting crops, abstracting infants or young people, spiriting away women after their accouchements, raising whirlwinds and storms, and often beating people most unmercifully. In fact, in former times, and even yet, in the islands of the extreme west, except from sheer old age, or some very ostensible cause, no one is ever believed to " die all out." True it is, that all the outward and visible signs of death are there—speech, motion, respiration, and sensation have ceased; the fountains of life are stopped, and heat has fled; the man is " cowld as a corpse; but what of that?—isn't it well known he got a *blast?* Sure 'tis no later than the day before yesterday week he was up and hearty, the likeliest boy in the parish, and there he is to-day as stiff as a peeler's ramrod. Didn't I see him with my two livin' eyes at Cormac Maguire's funeral, and he riding home fair and asey, the quitest baste that ever was crassed, without as much as a *deligeen bristoh** on him—and he, I may say, all as one as *black fasting;* † as he only tuck share of three half-pints at Tubber-na-Skollig—when the mare boulted at a wisp of straws that was *furlin* (whirling) at the cross-roads, and off she set, gal-lopin', gallopin', ever ever, till he fell on his head in the *shuch*‡ forninst his own door, and when they lifted him up he was speechless, and never tasted a bit of the world's bread from that day to this. The priest said an office for him, and the doctor said he was fractured; but sure everybody knows the good people had a hand in it."

Decomposition may indeed afford the physiologist proof positive that the vital spark has fled; but that avails little with a people who firmly believe that he is " with the fairies on the hill of Rawcroghan (Rath Croghan),§ or the Fort of Mullagha-

---

* *Deligeen bristoh:* A spur; literally " the thorn that incites."

† *Black fasting,* in the religious sense of the word, means total abstinence from meat and drink; but it is an expression not unfrequently applied in Connaught, to abstaining from whiskey. It is, however, generally used in a bantering sense.

‡ *Shuch,* the sink or stagnant pool of dirty water that is to be found opposite the entrance of the Irish cabin.

§ For a topographical and antiquarian description of the ancient palace of Rathcrogan, the Tara of the west, in the parish of Kilcorkey, near Ballynagar, county Roscommon, see Dr. O'Donovan's edition of the " Annals of the Four Masters," A.D. 1223, pp, 204, 205.

dooey,* where there's plenty of the neighbours gone afore him."
So rooted is this belief, that we have known food of different
kinds, bread, meat, and whiskey to be brought by the relatives
of deceased persons, and laid for weeks after in these places for
their comforts. Fairy-women are often employed to " set a
charm," and bargain for their release with the king and queen
of the *gentry*. Years may elapse, yet will the friends and rela-
tives still cling with desperate tenacity to the delusive hope
that the fairy-stricken will return; and they listen with avidity
to the various legends which tell how such and such of their
neighbours or friends in former times were seen in the court of
Fin Varra, or down in the Well of Oran, and sent home mes-
sages to their friends to be no ways uneasy about them, for
that they would return one day or another. But when the
death is very sudden, and no apparent cause can be assigned
for it, nothing will persuade the lower orders—and, during the
last century, not only the peasantry, but the middle and upper
classes—that the person has not been spirited away by super-
natural agency. The following historic Munster tale will illus-
trate this opinion better than any other which we can at pre-
sent remember :—

"In the year 1736, John, the son and heir of James Fitz-
gerald, was affianced to a young lady near Fermoy. Munster
did not produce in that day a man more noble in person, or with
more accomplished manners, or who more excelled in arms and
rural sports, than John Fitzjames. His betrothal and expected
wedding were the pleasing theme of conversation through the
country roads for weeks before the latter occurred, and heavy
and substantial were the presents and the contributions to the
festivities, sent in by the numerous and powerful friends of the
affianced parties, who themselves were to be guests on the
happy occasion. The wedding-day arrived, the knot was tied,
the feast concluded, and the music and dancing had com-
menced. The new-married couple were, as is usual, sent down

* Mullaghadooey, *mullach a dumha*, *i.e.*, the summit, or hill of the tumulus,
or sepulchral mound; a very remarkable conical hill, in the parish of Baslick,
and barony of Ballintobber, near my native village of Castlerea, county Ros-
common.

first in the country dance, and never, perhaps, in Munster, nor Ireland itself, did chanter and bow give forth a merrier strain, or timed the dance of a nobler pair than John Fitzjames and his blooming bride; and so thought all who had the happiness to witness them. In the height of his pride and joy, and in the heat of the dance, when he had gone down the middle and up again, changed sides and turned his partner with five-and-forty couple, John Fitzjames clasped his beautiful bride in his arms, impressed a burning kiss upon her lips, and as if struck by a thunderbolt, dropped dead at her feet! The consternation and horror which seized all present were indescribable; every means was adopted to restore animation; but John Fitzjames arose no more. For months and years after, the most reputed fairy-men and women throughout Munster were retained by his own and his virgin bride's friends, in the fruitless endeavour to bring him back from fairyland, whither it was universally believed he had been carried."

Our esteemed friend, Mr. Eugene Curry, to whom we are indebted for this and other tales, has kindly afforded us the following additional notice:—

"There are many mournful elegies in the Irish language still extant, which were written on John Fitzjames at the time of his decease, the best of which is that by James Fitzgerald. Among the many persons who repaired to Glinn to make battle with the fairies, were *Caitileen Dubh Keating*, and her daughter, *Caitileen Oge*, from Killclocher, near Loophead, in the county Clare. Caitileen Dubh and her daughter repaired from Glinn to Carrig Cliodhna* (Cleena's Rock), near Fermoy, where Cleena, the fairy queen of south Munster, was said to reside in her invisible palace. Here Caitileen, who *tarred* her clothes and rolled herself in feathers of various colours, met the queen face to face, and reproaching her with the abduction of John Fitzjames, demanded his restoration. Her majesty acknowledged the soft impeachment, but peremptorily refused to restore so noble a prize to any mere creature

---

* *Carrig-Cleena* is in the parish of Kelshannick, barony of Duhallow, county Cork. There is another Carrig-Cleena near the loud surge of Cleena's wave, in the vicinity of Glandore. See "Annals of the Four Masters," A.D. 1557, p. 1549.

of earth. A long argumentation then ensued between them on the matter, which ended, however, in the defeat of Caitileen and her daughter by the superior power of Cleena, who is one of the Tuatha de Dannan race, and whose history is preserved in the Book of Lismore, one of the ancient Irish manuscripts in the collection of the Royal Irish Academy. The whole of the argument between the queen and Caitileen was by Fitzgerald cast into a very curious and amusing Irish poem, which is still preserved in the county of Limerick, and of which I possess a fragment. The following rough, but literal translation, is a specimen of one of the stanzas :—

> " ' O Cleena, Christ himself salute thee!
>   Long is the journey I have made to thee,
>   From Cill Cluhar of the ripe berries,
>   And from Shannon's bank, where sail the swift ships :
>   Look down, and quickly inform me
>   What is the state of John Fitzjames?
>   Or has he parted with Isabel Butler ?
>   Or has he married the maid with the flowing hair ? ' "

To this Cleena answers

> " ' To marry or wed I shall not allow him :
>   I prefer, even tho' dead, to have him myself,
>   Than married to any beauteous maid of Erin ;
>   And here now, Caitileen, is thy information.' "

We remember a lady of wealth and high respectability in Connaught, who, having lost several of her children in succession, dedicated her next born son to the Virgin, and dressed him completely in white from top to toe, hat, shoes, and all, for the first seven years of his life. He was not allowed even to mount a dark-coloured horse, but had a milk-white pony for his own use. In this instance, however, the people's prediction, that there was " no use in going agin the *good people*," literally occurred ; for when he grew up to manhood, he met a sudden death—having died from the effects of a fall from his horse..

Whenever the slightest accident takes place, as when one falls, or even trips in walking, or sneezes,* it is attributed to the fairy influences by which the person is at that moment

* Sneezes. For some curious authorities respecting the superstitious belief about sneezing, see the "Irish Nennius," p. 145, note z.

supposed to be surrounded, and therefore it is expedient immediately to cross one's-self, and invoke a benediction. It would be considered not only disrespectful, but very unlucky, if the bystander did not say, "God bless you," or "God between you and all harm," or spit on you in such a case. *

It would be a difficult task to reduce to precise terms all the popular ideas on Irish pantheology, and as they can only be gleaned and sifted from the tale, the rite, or legend, they are best expressed by the same means. The general belief, however, is, that the "good people" or the "wee folk," as they are termed in Ulster, are fallen angels, and that their present habitations in the air, in the water, on dry land, or under ground, were determined by the position which they took up when first cast from heaven's battlements. These are almost the very words used by the peasantry when you can get one of them to discourse upon this forbidden subject. They believe that God will admit the fairies into his palace on the day of judgment, and were it not for this that they would strike or enchant men and cattle much more frequently. They sometimes annoy the departed souls of men who are "putting their pains of purgatory *over them*" on the earth.† The idea of their being *fallen angels*, came in with Christianity. In the "Book of Armagh" they are called "*the gods of the earth*"; and in the "Book of Lismore" they are described as the spirits or rather the immortal bodies and souls of the Tuatha de Dananns. The popular impression is, that the great majority of them are old, ugly, and decrepit, but have a power of taking on many forms, and that they generally assume a very diminutive size. It is also believed that they can at will personify or take on the shape of men or animals when they reveal themselves to human beings. The latter is not now, however, so generally believed as in former times, but there are still well-established visitations of both good and bad

---

* Spitting forms the most general, the most popular, and most revered superstition now remaining in Ireland. It is the great preservation against the Evil Eye, and the cure by the "fasting spittle" is one of the most widely-spread of all our popular antiquities ; therefore it shall in due course have a chapter devoted to its consideration.

† See the Life of Cairbre Crom, in Colgan.

people in the shape of black cats, which constantly appear to the faithful in this description of folk's lore.

It is a fact strange, but nevertheless true, that, according as the people are forgetting how to talk Irish, and have taken to reading Bibles and learning English, and thus losing the poetic fictions of other times, so have the animals which used in former days to be excessively communicative, given over holding any discourse with human beings. We must, therefore, go back to the ancient records for any well-authenticated instance of this description, and no better can be got than the following: In the "Wonders of Ireland," according to the Book of Glendalough, it is related, that "on a certain day the poet Mac Coise was at the Boyne, where he perceived a flock of swans, whereupon he threw a stone at them, and it struck one of the swans on the wing. He quickly ran to catch it, and perceived that it was a woman. He inquired tidings from her, and what it was had happened unto her, and what it was that sent her thus forth? And she answered him, 'In sickness I was,' said she, 'and it appeared to my friends that I died, but really it was demons that spirited me away with them.' And the poet restored her to her people." This is said to have occurred about the middle of the tenth century, the time when the elder Mac Coise, chief poet to O'Rourke, prince of Briefny, flourished.[*]

The "Book of Glendaloc" does not now exist; but a transcript of its "wonders" is preserved in the "Book of Ballymote," in the library of the Royal Irish Academy.

The belief in the *brownie* still remains among the superstitious Presbyterians of the mountains of Derry and Antrim, who leave bread and milk for him on the hearth at night. It is, however, very difficult to find any genuine pagan Irish superstition without being more or less modified by the wonders of the Old or New Testament. The witch of Endor, and the rod of Moses turned into the serpent, have modified many of our superstitions—the marvellous corrupting the marvellous. The devils going into the swine have also helped to tinge many of our saints' legends.

* See "The Irish version of Nennius," by the Rev. Dr. Todd, in the "Irish Archæological Society's Transactions," page 209.

The only genuine stories we have are told in the "Discourse between Patrick and Caoilte Mac Ronan," a purely bardic production, which has not been interpolated by the monks. In all the lives of Patrick he is made greater than Christ, and therefore his miracles become ridiculous.

The following instance of popular superstitious prejudice has been afforded the writer by a person who was present at the transaction; and, as it is best expressed in the words of the narrator, it is here inserted as a quotation: "I well remember in the year 1818, that Mary, the wife of Daniel Kelly, a bouncing, full, auburn-haired, snow-white-skinned woman, about twenty-eight years of age, died suddenly on a summer's day, while in the act of cutting cabbages in her garden. Great was the consternation throughout the entire parish of Moyarta, in the south-west of Clare, at this sad event, the more particularly as several persons who were in a westerly direction from her at the time, declared that they had *seen* and felt a violent gust of wind pass by and *through* them in the exact direction of Kelly's house, carrying with it all the dust and straws, &c., which came in its way. This confirmed the husband and friends of the deceased in their impression that she had been carried off to nurse for the fairies. Immediately Mary Quin, alias the Pet (*Maire an Pheata*), and Margaret MacInerheny, alias Black Peg, two famous fairy-women in the neighbourhood, were called in, who, for three days and three nights, kept up a constant but unavailing assault on a neighbouring fort or rath for the recovery of the abducted woman. But at the end of that time it was found that the body, or what in their belief appeared to be the body, of Mary Kelly, could not be kept over ground, wherefore it was placed in the grave, but still with a total unbelief of its identity. Her bereaved husband and her brothers watched her grave day and night for three weeks after, and then they opened it, in the full conviction of finding only a birch broom, a log of wood, or the skeleton of some deformed monster in it. In this, however, they were mistaken, for they found in it what they had put into it, but in a much more advanced state of decomposition."

Whenever the good people venture abroad, or suddenly

change their residence in the open day, their transit is marked by a whirlwind, in the eddies of which dust, straws, and other light substances, are taken up and carried along. When such occur, the Irish peasant, if conversing, ceases to speak, crosses himself, holds his breath, looks down, and mentally repeats a short prayer; and no irreverent expression with regard to the supernatural movement ever drops from him. Many persons have told us that they have often heard and FELT the fairies pass by them with a sound like that of a swarm of bees, or a flock of sparrows on the wing. An instance of this occurred lately during the hurricane at Limerick.

There is no prejudice more firmly rooted than the belief in the abduction of recently-confined females, for the purpose of acting as nurses either to the children of the fairy queen, or to some of those carried away from earth. In certain cases of mental aberration which sometimes occur at this period, the unhappy state of the patient is always attributed to fairy interference. It is believed that the real person is not physically present, but that the patient is one of the fairies who has assumed the features and general appearance of the abducted individual, while the actual person is " giving the breast" to one of Fin Varra's children in the fairy halls of the hill of Knockmaah, in the county Galway. In such cases, if there has been any delay in recovery, the medical attendant is at once discarded, and if a friar had been called in to read prayers over her, and that this did not prove immediately effectual, all legalised practitioners, medical or ecclesiastical, are dismissed, and the fairy doctor is applied to. His mode of proceeding is usually as follows: he fills a cup, or wine-glass with oaten meal, and mutters over it an Irish prayer. He then covers it with a cloth, and applies it to the heart, back, and sides, repeating the incantation on each application. If it is a fairy that is present, one-half of the meal disappears at one side of the vessel, as if it were cut down from above. That which remains is made into three small cakes and baked upon the hearth. The sick person is to eat one of these every morning, " fasting;" when the spell is broken, the fairy departs, and is once more replaced by the real mortal, sound and whole.

The "meal cure" is likewise employed, with some modification, for the heart-ache, and in that case, the expression, "*Foir an Cridhe*,—ease the heart, ease the heart," is made use of by the charmer on each application. The patient generally visits the doctor on a Monday, Thursday, and Monday, and the meal in the cup is lessened each time in proportion to the amount of disease removed, until at last the vessel is completely emptied. The remnant is brought home each day by the patient, who must not lose any of it, nor speak to any person by the way. The invalid then makes it into a cake, and sits by the fire until it is baked, taking care that neither cat, dog, nor any other living thing passes between him and his cake until it is baked and eaten with three sprigs of watercress, in the name of the Trinity. The meal cure is a very good specimen of fairy sleight of hand, and worthy the attention of modern wizards.

As the person is not always conscious of her state while labouring under what is termed by physicians, "puerpural mania," it is rather difficult to get any very accurate or collected account of the fairy nursery in which they pass their time; and when the cures and charms prove ineffectual, and they " die all out," the truth becomes more difficult to attain; nevertheless it is not quite impossible. In proof of this, we would refer our readers to a very poetic and well-told legend in the Rev. Mr. Neilson's "Introduction to the Irish Language,"[*] where we have an account of one Mary Rourke, who, having died in childbirth, in the county of Galway, was washed, laid out, waked, keened, and buried with all due form and ceremonial. Mary, however, " was in Knockmagha, three quarters of a year, nursing a child, entertained with mirth and sweet songs; but notwithstanding, she was certainly in affliction. At length the host of the castle told her that her husband was now married to another woman, and that she should indulge no longer in sorrow and melancholy; that Fin Varra and all his family were about to pay a visit to the province of Ulster. They set out at cock-crowing, from smooth Knockmaah forth, both Fin Varra and his valiant host. And many a fairy castle, rath

* Dublin, printed for P. Hogan, 1808.

and mount they shortly visited from dawn of day till fall of night, on beautiful winged coursers :—

> 'Around Knock Greine and Knock-na-Rae,
> Ben Bulbin and Keis-Corainn,
> To Ben Echlann and Loch Da éan,
> From thence north-east to Slieve Guilin,
> They travelled the lofty hills of Mourne,
> Round high Slieve Donard and Ballachanèry,
> Down to Dundrim, Dundrum and Dunardalay,
> Right forward to Knock-na-Feadala.' "

These are all the celebrated haunts of the fairy people in the west and north. Now at the foot of Knock-na-Feadala there lived with his mother, who was a widow woman, a boy named Thady Hughes, an honest, pious, hard-working bachelor. Well, Thady went out on Hallow Eve night, about the very time that the court of Fin Varra were passing through the air, and as he stood in the gap of an old fort looking up at the stars that were shining bright through the clear frosty air, he observed a dark cloud moving towards him from the south-west, with a great whirlwind; and he heard the sound of horses upon the wind, as a mighty troop of cavalry came over the ford, and straight along the valley, to the very rath on which he stood. Thady was in a mighty flustrification, and trembled all over; but he remembered that he had often heard it said by know-ledgable people, that if you cast the dust that is under your foot against the whirlwind at the instant that it passes you, "them that's in it" (that is, if they have any human being along with them) are obliged to be released. So, being of a humane disposition, he lifted a handful of the gravel that was under his foot, and threw it lustily, in the name of the Trinity, against the blast, when, lo and behold! down falls a young woman, neither more nor less than Mary Rourke from Galway, all the way; but mighty wake entirely. Thady took courage, having heard her groan like a Christian, so he spoke softly to her, and lifted her up, and brought her home to his mother, who took care of her till she recovered. In process of time the heart of Thady was softened, and he took Mary to wife, and they lived mighty happy and contented for a year and a day, the lovingest couple in the whole county Down, till a stocking merchant from Connemara, passing that way, recognized her as the wife of Michael Joyce, of Gort, who shortly after came all the ways from Connaught to claim her: and it took six clergy and a bishop to say whose wife she was.*

A few, however, of those who have been carried away have returned, and have left us faithful records of all they saw, and what was said and done in the court of his elfin majesty.

There lived a woman in Innis Shark—one of the group of islands on the eastern coast—named Biddy Mannion, as handsome and likely a fisherman's wife as you would meet in a day's walk. She was tall, and fair in the face, with skin like an egg, and hair that might vie with the gloss of the raven's wing. She was married about a twelvemonth, when the midwife presented her husband, Patsy-Andrew M'Intire, † with as fine a man-child as could be found between Shark and America, and sure they are the next parishes, with only the Atlantic for a mearing between them. The young one throve apace, and all the women and gossips said that Biddy Mannion was the lucky woman, and the finest nurse seen in the island for many a day. Now the king of the fairies had a child about the same age, or a little older; but the queen was not able to nurse it, for she was mighty weakly after her lying-in, as her husband had a falling-out with another fairy potentate that lives down one side of the Giant's Causeway, who, by the force of magic and *pishrogues*, banished the suck from the Connaught princess for spite. The gentry had their eye upon Biddy Mannion for a long time, but as she always wore a *gospel* round her neck, and kept an *errub* and a bit of a burnt sod from St. John's Night sewed up in her clothes, she was proof against all their machinations and seductions. At long run, however, she lost this herb, and one fine summer's night the young *gaurlough*,‡ being mighty cross with the teeth, would n't sleep in the cradle at all, but was evermore

* For further particulars on the subject of Irish medical superstitions, as regards the obstetric art, see the Author's essay on the subject in the "Edinburgh Monthly Journal of Medical Science," for May, 1849.

+ Patsy, Pad, Paddy, Parra, Pauric, Paddeny, Paurikeen, and Pandeen, are all abreviations, synonymes, or short names derived from Patrick, our patron saint.

‡ A very young infant.

starting and crying, as if the life was leaving him, so she got up at last, determined to take him to bed to herself, and she went down to the kitchen to light a candle. Well, just as she was blowing a coal, three men caught a hold of her, before she could bless herself, and she was unable to shout or say a word, so they brought her out of the house quite easy, and put her upon a pillion, behind one of themselves, on a fine black horse that was ready waiting outside the door. She was no sooner seated behind one of the men than away they all galloped, without saying a word. It was as calm and beautiful a night as ever came out of the sky, just before the moon rose " between day and dark," with the gloom of parting twilight softening every break upon the surrounding landscape, and not a breath of air was to be felt. They rode on a long time, and she did n't know where they were going to; but she thought to herself they must be on the mainland, for she heard the frogs croaking in the ditches, the *bunnaun lena* was sounding away in the bogs, and the *minnaun airigh* * was wheeling over their heads. At last the horse stopped of itself all of a sudden before the gate of a "big house," † at the butt of a great hill, with trees growing all round it, where she had never been before in her life. There was much light in the house, and presently a grand looking gentleman dressed all in scarlet, with a cocked hat on his head and a sword by his side, and his fingers so covered with rings that they shone "like *lassar lena* in a bog-hole," ‡ lifted her off the pillion as polite as possible, handed her into the house, and bid her a *cead mile failte*, just the same as if he had known her all his lifetime.

* There are no frogs in these small islands. The *Bunnaun lena* is the bittern, and the *Minnaun airigh* (the airy kid) is the clocking snipe, so called from the noise which it makes, like the bleating of a kid, while wheeling in the air during the twilight of a summer's evening. Neither of these birds are found in the small islands of the west.

† The word "big house" is applied by the peasantry to most gentlemen's seats.

‡ This, though a homely simile, is one very frequently used in many parts of Connaught, to express any bright shining appearance. The *Lassar lena*, which grows in bogs and marshy places, is the ranunculus flammea, so called from its brilliant yellow colour. It is a plant possessing many medicinal virtues, and will claim a special notice when we come to treat of the herb cures, and popular botany of the Irish.

The gentleman left her sitting in one of the rooms, and when he was gone she saw a young woman standing at the *thrashal* of the door, and looking very earnestly at her, as if she wanted to speak to her. " Troth I'll speak, any way," says Biddy Mannion, "for if I didn't, I'm sure I'd burst." And with that she bid her the time of day, and asked her why she was looking at her so continuously. The woman then gave a great sigh, and whispered to her, " If you take my advice, Biddy Mannion, you'll not taste bit, bite, or sup, while you are in this house, for if you do you'll be sorry for it, and maybe never get home again to your child or husband. I ate and drank my fill, *forrior geraugh*,* the first night I came, and that's the reason that I am left here now in this enchanted place, where everything you meet is bewitched, even to the mate itself. But when you go home send word to them that's after me, Tim Conneely, that lives one side of the Killaries, that I am here, and may be he'd try what Father Pat Prendergast, the blessed abbot of Cong, could do to get me out of it."

Biddy was just going to make further inquiries, when in the clapping of your hand the woman was gone, and the man with the scarlet coat came back, and the same strange woman, bringing a young child in her arms. The man took the child from the woman, and gave it to Biddy to put it to the breast, and when it had drank its *fill* he took it away, and invited her into another room, where the queen—a darling, fine-looking lady, as you'd meet in a day's walk—was scated in an arm-chair, surrounded by a power of quality, dressed up for all the world like judges with big wigs, and red gowns upon them. There was a table laid out with all sorts of eating, which the man in the cocked hat pressed her to take. She made answer that she was no ways hungry, but that if they could give her a cure for a little girl belonging to one of her neighbours, who was mighty *dauny*, and never well in herself since she had a fit of the *feur-gurtagh*,† while crossing the Minaune Pass in Achill,

---

* *Forrior geraugh*, literally, bitter grief, woe, or sorrow ; it is an expression denoting great regret.

† *Feur gortac*, literally, " *the hungry grass*," a weakness, the result of sudden hunger, said to come on persons during a long journey, or in particular places,

and to send herself home to Shark, she would be for ever obliged to them.   The king, for that was the gentleman with the cocked hat, said he had ne'er a cure.

" Indeed, then," said the mother of the child, " as I was the cause of your coming here, honest woman, you must get the cure ; go home," says she, speaking for all the world like an Englishwoman, " and get ten green rishes from the side of the well of Aughavalla,* throw the tenth away,† and squeeze the juice of the rest of them into the bottom of a taycup, and give it to the colleen to drink, and she will get well in no time."

The king then put a ring on her finger and told her not to lose it by any manner of means, and that as long as she wore this ring no person could hurt or harm her.   He then rubbed a sort of an ointment on her eyes, and no sooner had he done so than she found herself in a frightful cave where she couldn't see her hand before her.   "Don't be any ways afeard," says he; " this is to let you know what kind of a people we are that took you away.   We are the fallen angels that the people up above upon the earth call the fairies ;" and then after a while she began to see about her, and the place was full of dead men's bones, and had a terrible musty smell ; and after a while he took her into another room where there was more light, and here she found a wonderful sight of young children, and them all blindfolded, and doing nothing but sitting upon *pookauns.* ‡ These were the souls of infants that were never baptised, and are believed " to go into naught."   After that he showed her a beautiful garden, and at the end of it there was a large gate, which he opened with a key that was hung to his watch-chain. " Now," says he, " you are not far from your own house ;" so

in consequence of treading on a particular kind of *fairy-enchanted* grass, called the ꜰéaɲ ʒoɲċaċ by the native Irish.   A bit of oaten-cake is said to be the best cure for it.

* A holy well in the barony of Murrisk, not far from Croagh Patrick, celebrated for its "cures," and its blessed trout.

† The antiquity of tithes is instanced in numberless examples in our "cures" and fairy lore.   For example, ten gooseberry thorns are plucked to cure "the stye," nine are pointed at the part affected, and the tenth thrown over the left shoulder.   Nine was the mystic number; but the additional one was added by the church for wise purposes.

‡ *Pookauns,* mushrooms, fairy-stools, or puff-balls; the term is applied to all the family of fungi.

he let her out; and then says he, " who is that that is coming down the boreen;" and when she turned her back to look who it was, behold the man with the red coat and the cocked hat had disappeared.

Biddy Mannion could not see anybody, but she knew full well the place where she was in a minute, and that it was the little road that led down to the *annagh* * just beside her own house, and when she went up to the door she met another woman the very *moral* of herself, just as fair as if she saw her in the looking-glass, who said to her as she passed, " What a *gomal* your husband is that didn't know the difference between you and me."   She said no more, but Biddy went in and found her child in a beautiful sleep, with his face smiling, like the buttercups in May.

**Annagh*, a cut away bog.

INDEX.

—◆—